FAITH

IS THE VICTORY

Blessing!
Blessings!!

Ron Pegg

RON PEGG

Printed in Canada

ISBN: 978-1-4866-2001-2
eBook ISBN: 978-1-4866-2002-9

Word Alive Press
119 De Baets Street Winnipeg, MB R2J 3R9
www.wordalivepress.ca

Cataloguing in Publication information can be obtained from Library and Archives Canada.

CONTENTS

PREAMBLE

Each of us was created as a unique individual. There is no other human being exactly like you. God has no grandchildren. He just has children. Each individual has the choice to become an adopted child, a brother or sister of Jesus. With the freedom of will that each has, a person may also reject becoming part of the Family of God.

As I begin writing this book in late February 2019, I am very blessed to have fourteen grandchildren who are all in the early stages of life. A number have already accepted Jesus as Lord and Saviour. Isa and Torin are just two of whom, in their young teenage years, grasped onto an opportunity of preaching the gospel of Jesus. Others have been part of praise groups.

However, it is up to each of the fourteen as individuals to dedicate their lives to Him.

Each has the ultimate decision to make of moving over to the passenger seat and giving Jesus and the Holy Spirit the keys to run their lives.

This book is dedicated to each of these fourteen grandchildren:

Kaden

Daniel

Torin

Mia

Isa
Gabriella
Trenton
Aly
Joshua
Landon
Victoria
Chaim
Zadok
Nicklas

****

Special thanks to Sandra Batchelor & Jeff Wilson

INTRODUCTION

The Pegg family were Quakers in the Cromar area of east England. This was an area where brickmaking was very important. In the mid 1650s Oliver Cromwell had come to power. He had no love for the Quakers.

Members of the Pegg family followed William Penn to the area of Philadelphia in the very early stages. Penn was establishing a place in this new land that he had been given where there was to be complete religious freedom. Danial Pegg is recorded to have built the first brick house in this emerging city. It became the home of William Penn.

The city grew rapidly, as not only English settlers arrived, but also people of various Christian faiths from various European countries. The rapidly growing city was not developing a lifestyle that the Peggs liked. As a result, within a half a century this Quaker family was moving out into New Jersey, where there was more of a rural life. It was also a part of the land granted to William Penn.

It was just over one hundred years after the Peggs had come to the area of Philadelphia that the American war of independence was fought. The war caused major problems for the Quakers. Quakers do not believe in war. As a result, a number of their neighbours felt that these Quakers were opposed to their fight for independence. These neighbours felt that these Quakers were English Empire loyalists. Some of the Quakers were arrested and had their land and possessions taken from them.

Some of the Pegg clan joined other Quakers who were following a wagon trail to the future Canada. They were leaving the Philadelphia area. The name Philadelphia, which William Penn had chosen, comes from the Book of Revelation, the last book in the Bible written by John.

John was describing the seven churches found on the peninsula of Greece. The church of Philadelphia was the sixth church that he described. It was the church of a group of believers who were hard workers. Despite their hard work, the people of this church did not prosper, but always got by and were faithful. This is an almost perfect description of the Pegg clan.

When the Peggs and their Quaker brothers arrived in the future Canada, they settled on land just north-east of the area that became Newmarket.

It seemed that these humble Christians had been on a continuous journey since they left England in the mid-1660s, until 1804, the year they claimed their new home in what was soon to become Canada.

It was Isaac Pegg who brought his family on this last part of the journey. Samuel Pegg, my great great grandfather, was a young boy who walked behind his father's wagon on this journey.

———————

Ron Pegg writes a weekly column Letters from Ron, for the Dundalk Herald and Advance.

The article - which is a volunteer contribution - is usually found on the paper's Church Page.

A number of these Letters are found throughout this book.

CHAPTER 1

"A HERITAGE OF FAITH"

I was born on March the seventh, 1938. I had three older sisters. Norma, the youngest, was still seven years older than I. Dad had become a baker in Beeton, Ontario. Upon my birth, a number of the people said to Dad, he finally had "his baker." This was an age when sons followed in their father's footsteps.

On the other hand, my mother had a desire to have a preacher as a son. She almost named me Clinton after her favourite radio preacher, Clinton Churchill, from the Churchill Tabernacle in Buffalo New York.

My Mother was born into a family with a rich Christian heritage.

Her grandfather on her mother's side, Emmanuel Brown, was a lay supply preacher who spoke a number of times at the Hartman Methodist Church situated just south of Mount Albert. It is just six miles from where the Pegg clan settled in 1804. As it happened, I later had the opportunity of speaking at the Church, which in 1925 had become a United Church. I spoke there in 1957. Wes Theaker, the area's undertaker was present. Previously, he had heard my great grandfather Brown speak. It was a humbling experience for me to meet this man.

Mother's father was the Sunday School Superintendent. My Mother adored her father - and it seemed that my grandfather had a special place in his heart for his young daughter, Flossie Pearl.

The family of Isaac Pegg attended this same Hartman Church. This is where Dad and Mom's love grew. It was 1922. Mom and Dad were not married, but Mom was expecting her first child who would become Ruby Bernice.

To have the Sunday School's Superintendent's daughter pregnant and not married was a local scandal. A few of the self-righteous women in the church spoke unkind words about Mom. She heard those remarks. She lost all desire to attend church. She never got over this. She married Dad before Bernice was born. In her life, Bernice became her church's organist for over twenty-five years.

Although Mother did not attend church, her love for Jesus and her Heavenly Father just continued to grow and grow. Her own father continued to love his daughter with a passion that only a father can have for his daughter.

The family that Mother married into, the Pegg family who had come to Canada as Quakers, had moved east of Mount Albert in the mid-1850s. They had lost contact with their Quaker base. This was the time of the Methodist circuit riders, who were followers of John Wesley. The Peggs had become Methodists, who eventually attended the newly built Hartman Church.

Although they had become Methodist, their branch of the Pegg clan continued in the heritage of their forefathers. They were hard working people who were good citizens and quietly followed their faith.

CHAPTER 2

THE EARLY YEARS

The home that I was born into was, on the surface, a typical family of the 1940s. However, just the same as every human has been created as a unique individual, every family is a unique family.

My dad was different than most of his brothers. His father married a young Irish lass with the last name of Dunn. She had recently come to Canada. For most of my life, I have believed that my heritage was primarily English, because of the Pegg and Brown background.

I was over sixty-five years of age when we took a couple of weeks holiday to Ireland. It was during this trip that I came to realize that Grandmother Dunn Pegg was the person from whom my dad received many of his genes. He passed these Irish genes onto my brother Dave, my sister Bernice, to me and to a much lesser degree, my sister Norma. In our own way, we each have enjoyed the stage and a microphone.

This explained why my Dad enjoyed wearing a costume, when a costume added to an evening of fun. It further explained why he was the producer of many three act plays. His sister and most of his brothers had inherited much more of their father's English characteristics.

I have also been influenced by my mother's love of Jesus Christ and her love of the scriptures of the Bible. Dad, in his faith, was much more inclined to be a typical Pegg, having major influences from their Quaker heritage. These people quietly wear their faith.

Dad went to the United Church in Beeton every Sunday night. Even as a small boy, I often went with him. My sisters sang in the choir. When I was old enough, I was taken to Sunday School on Sunday morning by my sisters Bernice and Marion. Both were teachers in the Sunday School. Dad would be at home sleeping after his long six days in the bakery and grocery store.

Mother made sure that we children were up and dressed. After we left, Mom would quickly get back to her radio to listen to Clinton Churchill. She had been up since dawn listening to different radio ministers. As Mother's children we had no idea why she didn't go to church. We never thought anything of it. I guess we knew that she was getting her teaching from the radio ministries. She was home to get us ready for Sunday School. She was home to have dinner (lunch) ready for us when we returned from Sunday School. She also prepared anything and everything for family visits to our cousins on Sunday afternoons.

One of my favourite pastimes was to play being a radio minister. I would get the piano stool and wind it up as high as it would go. I would get a broom from the broom closet and place it against the wall in front of the stool. It was my microphone. I would get a couple of hymn books from the top of the piano and place them on the stool. I would get my Bible. I was ready to preach.

———— LETTERS FROM RON ————

The gospel on my mother's radio has been a very positive influence in my life. On Sunday afternoon at three o'clock, Mom's radio would be tuned to the Barrie radio station. From Edmonton, Alberta came the broadcast called Canada's National Bible Broadcast. We were two of the two and a half million plus Canadians listening to this broadcast, as it was aired across Canada.

The preacher on the broadcast was Ernest Manning, who was also the premier of the province of Alberta. Mr. Manning was Premier for over twenty years. He never lost an election. He always had a majority. He retired undefeated. He left Alberta with no debt. He built many foundations that helped to make Alberta the prime province in Canada over the next five decades.

When someone challenged him about mixing politics and religion, his response was as follows. If he was forced to give up either the position of premier or his ministry, there would be no choice. He had been in the ministry much longer than he had been in politics. His ministry would continue.

He also stated that any legislation that was contrary to the Bible was not a good piece of legislation. It should never happen.

Mr. Manning's Social Credit Party has long since died. The Alberta of 2019 is not the prosperous province it once was.

As we are approaching the halfway point of 2019, Canada's National Bible Broadcast is on its ninety-fifth year of broadcasting. It is believed that the ninety-five years of broadcasting makes it the world's longest playing broadcast.

Its importance today is found more on the internet than live radio. One of Mr. Manning's sermons is still regularly broadcast on the program.

An example of the outreach of this broadcast is written about in one of the recent letters that the broadcast received. The letter was from a young girl in Nigeria. She had picked up the broadcast on the internet. Her school had just gone through a major crisis, which had led to the death of five students. The five had died with no hope. This young lady was deeply bothered by this event.

When she came across the "Back to the Bible" broadcast, she shared it with her friends, who shared it with their friends - and the sharing goes on. Two hundred and thirty-nine students accepted Jesus as Lord of their life. Many of this group now gather weekly in one of the schoolrooms, so that they may listen to the broadcast together.

The young girl's first name is Janet. She describes Canada's "Back to the Bible" broadcast in the following words. She states that the broadcast is a powerful, undiluted, undeniable, unfailing, true message of God's salvation.. Each of these students now knows that Jesus is the way, the truth and the life.

CHAPTER 3

"GIVING"

I was by now eight years old. People in Beeton had been hearing of a fire in Northern Ontario that completely destroyed a family home. They had not been able to save anything. My dad decided to put a box up in our store where people could place donations for this family. Dad planned to mail this box to the family.

Because the box was in our store and it had been set up by my dad. I was very aware of it. Children did not have many toys in the 1940s. One of my few toys was a little truck. As I write, I can still see this truck. It was a blue truck similar in style to a half ton. It was about five inches long, two inches wide and one and a half inches tall. It was by far my favourite toy.

As the days went by, my thoughts turned to putting the toy truck in the box for the little boy whose family had lost everything. It was a daily struggle for me. On the second last day the box was in Dad's store, I took my little truck and put it in. I have never regretted giving the little truck, but I have never forgotten it, or the joy I anticipated that little Northern Ontario boy had when he saw his new truck.

This happened in November. It was not long until Christmas. In our home on Christmas morning, each of us five children opened our gifts. The one from Santa Claus did not have any wrapping. As we were finishing unwrapping the gifts, there was a knock on the store door.

Dad went to answer. It was Walt Wallwin who lived by himself in a shack west of the village. Mr. Wallwin probably didn't even realize it was Christmas. Even if he did realize it was Christmas, he needed a few things from the store. He knew Garney Pegg would help him out.

It was now time to go to Grandma Boden's place in Mount Albert, which was twenty-five miles away. Before we left, Dad went about the store and filled up a box of groceries. We would drop it off at the Bemrose home, as a Christmas gift to this struggling family.

There is no question that it is more blessed to give than receive. We didn't know this, but according to the established lines of poverty, our family was below that line. Our favorite Sunday night dinner was Kraft dinner on toast. We always had enough to eat. Our clothes were clean. We had a roof over our head.

Our family was certainly not part of the village establishment, but we had our friends, our loyal customers and we had each other.

CHAPTER 4

OUR CHRISTIAN COMMUNITY

There were three churches in Beeton: The Church of England (Anglican), St. Andrews Presbyterian and Trinity United. Beeton, like most other places in the area, had its Orange Hall where the Orange Lodge met. To the west of Beeton was Colgan. Colgan was the centre of the Roman Catholic community.

The three churches in the village had their families from the village and the surrounding area. There were still problems between the United and the Presbyterians going back in time to 1925. The United Church had been formed in 1925, when the Methodist Congregational and Presbyterian Churches had joined together. However, portions of many Presbyterian congregations had independently voted to remain as a Presbyterian congregation. St. Andrews in Beeton was one of the churches who had voted to remain Presbyterian. Some of the members of St. Andrews left that church and became members of Trinity United. There were even families where some family members stayed at St. Andrews while others in the family went to Trinity. There were hard feelings. I had friends from school who were Presbyterian. They weren't even born when the new United Church began in the former Methodist Church. These Presbyterian friends would have nothing to do with Trinity United.

As an aside, when I was seventeen years of age, I preached one Sunday morning in the United Church and the next Sunday morning in the Presbyterian Church. I preached the same sermon from the same scriptures at both services. To the best of my knowledge, there were no problems.

In the winter time, there was a church hockey league where each of the churches played against each other. The competition was quite friendly.

The Orange Lodge was where the followers of King Billy met. The Orange Lodge was supposed to stand for religious freedom, but was in any case a struggle between Roman Catholics and Protestants. Each year on July 12th, the members of the Orange Lodge celebrated their victory in Ireland in the 1600s. There was an annual large Orange parade on that day. It was held in Beeton on two different occasions.

The streets were crowded with people for the great parade, that had a number of pipe and drum bands as part of the celebration. This was considered to be a Protestant event. Roman Catholics were not involved. However, I have often heard my sisters laugh that at the evening dance, they danced with many boys from the Catholic community.

There were some very strong feelings. There were a number of weddings where the father of the bride did not attend, because his daughter was marrying a Catholic and the wedding was being held in the Catholic Church in Colgan.

In the case of our family, my Grandfather Boden had often played the role of King Billy, the leader of the war in Ireland. Every Orange Parade was led by King Billy. I observed the Orange Parade and found it exciting as a celebration. I never had any further involvement. Many of the boys with whom I played hockey and ball worshipped in Roman Catholic churches.

My Dad had bread routes that were on the roads of the Catholic community. Dad often stated that when you had a Roman Catholic on your route, you had a very loyal customer.

——— Letters from Ron ———

*My Grandmother Boden lived with my aunt in Mount Albert.
When Grandma was in her late 70s, she tripped into a hole in the
ground and broke her hip. She needed to have someone to look after
her each and every day. My aunt and her family were going on a
couple of weeks of holidays. My mother agreed that she, along with
my brother and myself, would go to look after Grandma.*

*On the second day that we were with Grandma, my mother
suggested that I get out my grandmother's Bible, with its big print
and ask her if she would like me to read to her. Grandma could see
a wee bit, but she was legally blind from an accident in which some
acid was spilled in her eyes.*

*Grandma said that she would enjoy me reading to her and
suggested that I should read from the Psalms. She loved the Psalms.
I never have forgotten this opportunity to read to my grandma. I
also have never forgotten her love of the Psalms. As the years have
passed by - over seventy years - I have developed a love for the Psalms
similar to the one Grandma had.*

*I have come to realize that the Psalms are very much about
relationships with God - make a joyful noise unto the Lord - I
will lift up my eyes unto the hills; the best known one, the 23rd
Psalm - the Lord is my shepherd - which has at least six important
statements about Jesus the Shepherd, and me, the lamb. Yes, Psalm
after Psalm are love letters illustrating how our relationship with
our Holy God should be. A person cannot read the Psalms often
enough. It is possible to read the book of Psalms in a month by
reading five Psalms plus every day. This can be repeated month after
month. Every time that you read through Psalms, your knowledge
and understanding of this love relationship will grow.*

*As a teenager, I purchased a booklet that contained the book of
Proverbs. By reading one chapter a day for a month, one can almost
read through this entire book. This book is about the relationship
each of us has with our fellow man. It talks of the importance of
marrying a good woman, the importance of being wise in the use of*

alcohol, paying attention to a Godly Father's instructions, to follow love and faithfulness, that the fear of the Lord is the beginning of wisdom, the fruit of righteousness is a tree of life, a generous person will prosper, and whoever loves discipline loves knowledge. These are but a few of the pieces of advice found in Proverbs.

CHAPTER 5

"SCHOOL DAYS"

It was September 1943. I was five and a half years old. School had started the previous day. The boys that I played with were either six years old or about to turn six. They had all begun school the previous day. My Mother asked me if I wished to go to school, because my best friends were in school. I decided that I wanted to go. In the year 2019, I would not even have been allowed to start.

My sister Bernice would take me to school. My teacher was Mrs. Hall, who attended Trinity United as we did. She was a friend of the family. Mrs. Hall continued to be my teacher in Grade 2. When I graduated from grade one, my marks were second to last in my class. The last person failed.

Those of us who lived in the village usually went home for lunch, as did Mrs. Hall. It was early in the spring. I was returning to school after lunch. Mrs. Hall was also returning. I walked with her. When I got to school, some of the older boys had some pen nibs. To write in ink, it was necessary to fix the nib onto a pen stick to dip into an inkwell. The older boys gave some of these sharp pen nibs to us younger ones, telling us to jab other kids with them. I began doing this and was having fun with my fellow "jabbers". Mrs. Hall came out of the school and caught us. She took away our little weapons, giving them to the students who had just been jabbed, instructing them to jab those who they had just been jabbed by. One boy I had jabbed enjoyed this very much, jabbing me much harder than I jabbed him.

When recess came, he was in the washroom at the same time as me. He couldn't resist asking me how I liked the jab. I replied by cursing the teachers. He said that he was going to tell Mrs. Hall, which he did. When I returned to the classroom, Mrs. Hall called me up to her desk. She asked me if I had said what she had been told I had. My reply was that I had. Mrs. Hall then gave me the strap and made me stand in the corner for the rest of the afternoon. I was afraid to go home. I went a couple of blocks to the chopping mill, then rode a couple of wagons that were going to and from the mill. It was almost six o'clock before I returned home.

When I arrived home, the family was sitting around the supper table. When I came in, they all smiled at me. In our small village, word had already reached them that I had received the strap.

I have never felt the same about Mrs. Hall since that day. I really felt - and still feel - that I should not have been punished with the strap. She had not herself heard me curse the teachers. She had not observed me. It was possible that I should have been put in the corner, but punishment by the strap seemed to me too harsh. I would have forgiven her had she admitted that she made a mistake, but the subject never came up again.

Just as I had reacted out of anger, Mrs. Hall - an adult - had also reacted out of anger. Do I Love Mrs. Hall? The answer is yes, but I have never forgotten the day that she gave me the strap.

CHAPTER 6

SCHOOL DAYS - CONTINUED

It was when I entered Grade four that I became a student of Miss Vera Hastings. Miss Hastings came from Tottenham. She changed my life. This young woman believed in stressing the importance of everyday performance. She had a system of giving stars for each task that her students performed. I became one of the top students in my class. She gave presents to her students for their achievements. Among the rewards that I received were my first Bible and a small book that told the Christmas story.

My penmanship was never good. In the second year that Miss Hastings taught us, I was determined to have my writing submitted to the Beeton Fall Fair and judged in a competition with other grade five students. I have no idea how many times I took my completed writing project up to Miss Hastings, only to have her tell me it wasn't good enough. Late in the school day, she accepted my project.

It was very interesting that the next day, I could not find my writing at the fair. It must have got lost!!!

The day after I completed grade five and summer vacation had begun, I lay on my bed and cried my eyes out, because Miss Hastings would no longer be my teacher. She didn't teach grade six, but even more significantly, she was moving to a different school.

Years later when I became a teacher, much of Miss Hastings' teaching style became the basis of my method of teaching.

Miss Hastings was a life changer.

And then there was Mr. George Cowan. Mr. Cowan was the school principal and became my teacher in grades six and seven.

Mr. Cowan was a small man in stature, but a giant of a man in character. He only stood five feet and (maybe) three inches tall.

He was not only a teacher at the school. He also taught girls in a class at our Sunday School. He sang in the choir and was a beautiful trumpet player. In other words, he influenced the entire community of Beeton.

One day, the entire school went to the arena for an hour of skating. Mr. Cliff English was the town foreman, who also looked after the arena. Most people called him "Cliff". On the day that we were skating, a number of the students called him "Cliff". When we returned to the school, Mr. Cowan gave us a short lecture, instructing us students not to call Mr. English, "Cliff", as we had not earned the right to do this. This little lecture has affected me ever since.

It is important that we honour our elders. The fifth commandment tells us to honour our father and mother, that their days on earth may be long and blessed. The extension of mother and father is our elders.

I spent many hours in the Beeton arena. In fact, when I left Beeton in 1965, I had spent more time in the Beeton arena than any other person, except Mr. English. I have never told anyone what to call me. There are former students who call me Mr. Pegg and those who call me Ron. Then, there are those who call me by some term of affection, such as 'Coach'. This is because to them, that is who I am. It is interesting to note that former students who always call me Mr. Pegg are usually students with whom I was - and still am - very close. Conversely, students with whom I was not involved to any extent have no problem calling me Ron.

Mr. Murray Juffs was my principal in Flesherton high school for a dozen years. He and I became best of friends. I miss him to this day. Even though we were the very best of friends, I always called him Mr.

Juffs. It still agitates me a little when I hear teachers who had never earned the right call Mr. Juffs, Murray.

Mr. Cowan taught us some gospel hymns in our music class. One of these hymns was "Dare To Be A Daniel". My first time preaching took place at the Ontario High School Athletic Camp just outside of Orillia. My theme was the chorus of this song, "Dare to be a Daniel, Dare to stand alone, Dare to have a purpose firm, Dare to make it known". The words of this song have gone long beyond that service. It has been an important theme in my life.

This gospel hymn is not found in many hymn books, but some Presbyterian churches have a hymn book containing it. I often choose this hymn as one of the hymns for any service I have the opportunity of speaking at, if "Dare to Be a Daniel" is part of the church's hymn book.

Then there was the day that we boys were playing soccer outside of the window of the grade one and two classroom. These classes were held in the basement of the school. It was recess time. The grade one and two teacher was Miss Olga Galbraith, a lifelong friend of my sister Bernice. Because of the noise we made, she came outside, asking us to go and play elsewhere.

The boys in charge of our game were the same boys who had given us the pen nibs back in grade two. They decided that we were not moving. In short order, Mr. Cowan was out the door and we were soon inside the classroom, sitting in our seats. After recess ended, Mr. Cowan gave us a lecture. He then proceeded to give the strap to all eight of us. I thought, "If I will get at the end of the line. Mr. Cowan will be worn out by the time he reaches me". He wasn't. He was just getting warmed up.

I have a completely different outlook to this implementation of the strap. I was guilty as charged. The strapping was well deserved. I have no negative thoughts about this event and came away with two very positive thoughts. Authority must be obeyed and it is not a good idea to follow the crowd.

CHAPTER 7

I HAVE BEEN "BORN AGAIN"

There are those people who will ask a person, "What is the day and the year that you were born again"? There are those people who can tell you the moment that he, or she, accepted Jesus Christ as their Lord and Saviour. There are those who would say that if you can't name a specific time, you are not then born again.

Just after my eleventh birthday, my Dad took Mother, David and I to Buffalo on a Saturday afternoon so Mother could visit the Churchill Tabernacle and it's pastor, Clinton Churchill. Mother had been listening to Mr. Churchill on the radio for years. We stayed overnight in a hotel less than a block from the church. We attended the service on Sunday morning. Our mother was very happy to have this experience.

After the service was over, we returned to Toronto to the Canadian National Exhibition grounds where a well known evangelist and faith healer, Oral Roberts, was holding a tent crusade. When Mr. Roberts gave the altar call, my brother and I both stood up. When Mr. Roberts gave the invitation to come forward, I was very hesitant to go. My little brother was insistent that we go, because we had stood up. We went forward to the altar and were accompanied in prayer in an area at the side of the tent, which had been set up for this purpose.

Was this the night when I was born again? It was certainly the night that I went down the aisle with my brother for the purpose of accepting

Jesus. I had many thoughts about this in the following days. I came to the conclusion that this was not the night.

Jesus had always been part of me for as long as I could remember. In a moment as a very young boy, Jesus had become part of me. I look at the Oral Roberts crusade as the night that I walked down the aisle as a witness for Jesus. I do not believe that this was the night that I was born again. That happened many years before the evening with Mr. Roberts. Jesus and I both know this is true. Jesus knows the moment. I don't.

This is the story of many Christians who grew up in a Christian home and environment. They just grew into being born again.

I have been in attendance at a church, where I have watched the same person go to the altar many, many times. I don't know their reasons.

On the other hand, I have been to a number of Billy Graham crusades and watched many of his other crusades on television. It always happens. When Billy gave the call, the Holy Spirit moved as a mighty wind. The people literally pour out of their seats and down the aisle. For the majority of the people, it is their first time to the altar. The great majority of these people have just been born again. Their lives have been changed forever because when Jesus comes a person's way, that person's life begins changing. Some change very quickly. Others are on a long journey of slow growth.

Let us not misunderstand the previous paragraph. Each "born again" person is certainly a babe in Jesus. Each of us needs to grow. I accepted Jesus as Lord and Saviour of my life over seventy-five years ago. I am still growing. I am still learning to lean on Jesus. I know that I will need to grow every day that I live. He, through the Holy Spirit, will be very important in helping with my growth.

CHAPTER 8

PASTOR HALL

The Orange Hall was just a couple of doors down the street from Trinity United Church. Like most Orange Halls, it was not very big, but was the place where many of our village activities took place.

When a movie projectionist came to town and was going to be sharing a series of movies over a number of Tuesdays, we kids were very excited, even when the projector, or movie, broke in the middle of the show. This event happened in the Orange Hall. When my two oldest sisters got married, the community showers were held in the Orange Hall, which was packed with people. An orchestra of saxophones, piano and drums provided dance music from the small stage.

Then there was Pastor Hall. He came from Kettleby on Sunday nights. I was around ten years of age, when the Pastor first came. The United Church had changed its main service from the evening to the morning.

Shortly after these weekly services had begun, I was in attendance. No one went with me. There were no other young people present. In truth, there were very few people at the services. Pastor Hall gave little prizes to new visitors who came. On one Sunday night, I took my mother. On another Sunday night my dad was my guest. Pastor Hall brought special speakers to try and increase the congregation. Nothing worked. I continued to attend for a number of months. I purchased one of their hymn books, which I still have.

Songs such as "Whiter Than Snow", "Shower of Blessings", and "There's Not a Friend Like the Lowly Jesus", became part of my life.

By the time spring had come, my attendance became irregular. By the time Pastor Hall held a service revival meeting in a tent at Beeton Park, I had practically stopped attending. I sensed Pastor Hall's disappointment in me. I think he blamed other people, but this was not the case. It was a decision made by me.

If Pastor Hall ever looks at this earth from Heaven, he must be amazed as how important his meetings in the Orange Hall were to my life's direction. I never realized it at the time. In fact, I didn't realize it until over twenty-five years later, that this was the beginning of my long growth to be aware of the Holy Spirit.

Pastor Hall also whetted my appetite for outreach and evangelism in the Christian Church.

His influence added to the foundation of evangelism that was at the heart of the gospel message my mother listened to.

CHAPTER 9

"PEOPLE"

One of my jobs in our grocery store and bakery was to ride my bike on Saturday mornings to various people's homes and get grocery orders. I would return to the store with these orders and the people working in the store would prepare the orders, then Dad delivered the orders in the afternoon.

One of the homes I went to belonged to the Riddles. In past generations, the Riddles had owned the farm just north of the village. They were Presbyterians. There were four in the present generation. None had married. The two sons had problems with their eyes. One of the boys and one of the girls had passed away. The remaining sister looked after her blind brother. The brother was always in the kitchen, when I went for the order. He loved to talk and to listen. When I was ready to go to university, he and his sister gave me their big family Bible. I just recently gave their Bible to our daughter.

Shortly after the time Pastor Hall had been in our village, Hazel McCague entered the life of our village and church as the recent bride of Elwood McCague. Mrs. McCague had attended the Avenue Road Church, which the popular Charles Templeton had been filling with young people. This was during the time Charles Templeton was compared to Billy Graham, as a great young evangelist. Mrs. McCague had also regularly attended the Peoples' Church, where Oswald J Smith was founder and pastor. Mr. Smith was a great friend of Mom's radio preacher, Clinton Churchill.

Mrs. McCague became very active in our church and Sunday School. She taught a teenager's Bible Class regularly attended by over fifteen of my friends. She always ended the class with a call for any of us who had not accepted Jesus as Lord and Saviour to accept Him. She never took for granted that all of her students had already made this choice. Her message of Salvation was much stronger than what was usual in the mid-1950s United Church.

Around the same time that Mrs. McCague came, Mr. and Mrs. L. O. Thornton retired to Beeton. Their background was very similar to Mrs. McCague. Mr. Thornton became very active in the Sunday School. When I became Sunday School Superintendent, he became my assistant. The advice he gave was very important to me. He would be critical of one, when he felt he needed to be. He helped to develop my leadership skills.

Many were the evenings that I went to the Thornton home for supper and an evening of fellowship. If I was speaking at one of the local church services, this couple would be there.

As a result of Mrs. McCague, the Thorntons and my mother's love of the gospel, my development as a member of the United Church was quite different than the development of many of our other young people.

One of the results of this was that I purchased many slides featuring gospel choruses for the Sunday School. We would show these slides on a screen and sing them, accompanied by Phyliss Reynold on the piano. Very few churches were using slides and choruses at this time.

CHAPTER 10

"METZ"

Although his family did attend the Anglican Church, I do not know what Metz Hills' relationship was with the Lord. What I do know is that Metz Hill has been a major influence on me.

Metz, whose real name was Earl, got the nickname "Metz" from the hockey playing Metz brothers of the 1940s Toronto Maple Leafs. Metz was an avid Leafs fan.

He probably would be classified as having special needs. A slow learner in the education system today.

I got to know Metz when I was still a small boy. He spent much of his time on benches and steps in front of Camplin's Store on the corner of Main and Centre streets, Beeton. This area was part of my playground. I often sat with him. His knowledge of sports teams and sports trivia was amazing. When a person from a small town in eastern Ontario came to Beeton, I would often hear Metz ask about famous ball or hockey players from that town. While not many people from outside a town would know, Metz would know all about said players. I witnessed this happening on three different occasions.

Metz looked after the village's bowling greens. He cut the grass, then rolled the greens and I sometimes helped. I would assist him if he was fixing a hole in the ball diamond screen, which was beside the bowling green.

Metz's full-time job was working the night shift at the Beeton Telephone Company. At that time, the operator took your call and connected you to the person you were calling. The phone company was not very busy at night. Metz could easily handle this job. When a hockey team from the village was playing an important game miles from Beeton, one of the coaches would call the phone company. If the Beeton team won, the coach would ask to be connected to 6 – 2. That meant Beeton had won 6 – 2. If the caller said he wanted to be connected to 2 – 6, that meant Beeton had lost 6 – 2. Anyone from Beeton could now call Metz, the night operator, then he in turn would give that person the score of the game. At the time, this was the only way that a person could get the score.

Metz often got a ride to Barrie to watch Hap Emms run a practice for the Barrie Flyers, at the time one of the best junior hockey teams in Canada.

When Beeton started up a midget hockey team, I was of that age group. Metz Hill became our coach.

What follows is one of the most interesting and significant happenings in my life. When we were in the dressing room and Metz was talking to us, most of the boys ignored him and even laughed at him. I did not. I listened as closely as I could to this man. I made a mental file of all he said. When I began coaching, it was Metz's ideas and drills that I used. I had no other background. Years later, when the Beeton hockey team that I was coached were Ontario finalists, the lessons that these young players were taught were based upon a foundation that Metz had developed in me.

The other boys didn't listen, but I did. This foundation had gone on to be a small part of Jimmy Rutherford's foundation as the general manager of the Pittsburgh Penguins - and now as a member of the Hockey Hall of Fame - and also our son Rob's baseball coaching at Vanguard University in Costa Mesa, California.

Many are the stories that we could tell of Metz.

As I wrote at the beginning of the chapter, I never knew what, if anything, made up Metz's faith. I just know that I am very thankful that my God placed Metz in a very significant role in my life.

Metz died a young man and unfortunately, I could not be in Beeton for his funeral. Jimmy Rutherford's mom and dad were among the six people attending.

Although Metz was laughed at by many, his contributions far outweighed the contributions of those who laughed and did not listen.

—— Letters from Ron ——

Although it seems that the world is in complete chaos, the God who made it is still very much in complete control.

The scene of God and the world can be compared to the mother who has one, two, or even four, or five young children in her home. When one enters this home, it may appear that the home is in complete chaos. Yet it is not. The very patient and loving mother is very much in charge. She patiently allows these young children to form a unique personality. Under the leadership of our Heavenly Father, this is called free will.

Our God has created each of us with a free will. The purpose of this is so each of us can develop individuality. However, God has a hidden agenda. He wants and craves for each of us to love Him. However, He wants us to do this because, as an individual, each of us wants to. He does not wish to have a robot's love. There would be no satisfaction in this.

Yes, His hidden motive is for each of us to take the individuality He gave us and give it back to Him, so that we can embody the complete joy He has for us, the individual that He has created.

Each of us can only have this great life by giving our individuality back to Him for Him to use.

My mother was a completely liberated woman. She never worked outside of our home. She never had a bank account of her own. She was always home when each of us five children lived at home, over a period of fifty years. She believed that the purpose given to her by her Heavenly Father, was to raise and help develop her five children. She never found any other major purpose. The Bible states that by their fruit, you shall know them.

In the Old Testament, we have the book of Esther. This book is the great story of a Jewish woman who was living under captivity in a foreign land. She ended up being married to the king of the land.

As queen, she found herself in a place where she needed to address the king, in order to save her Jewish brethren living under the king. In that day and age, the queen was to be seen, but not heard. In fact, if she spoke out to the king, the queen would be executed. Queen Esther did speak out. She was not executed. She was in God's place for the purpose of doing exactly what she did. She was created to save the Jewish people in that day and age.

Each of us individuals were created for a purpose by our own Heavenly Father. We can only achieve this purpose through Him.

CHAPTER 11

PRAYER

Our family always had a prayer before we ate dinner and supper (today called lunch and dinner). It was a blessing over our food. Mother was the person who always prayed. At bedtime, I was taught to kneel beside my bed and pray for the blessings of the day, for family and friends, for a good night's sleep and for the events of the coming day.

My mother believed strongly in the power of prayer. I travelled to Rochester New York as an eleven-year-old with Dad and Mom in order that Dad could be prayed for by Little David, a young lad who was a faith healer. Dad suffered from migraine headaches. We were leaving for Rochester at four in the morning so we could be in Rochester for the afternoon meeting. Dad went out to the garage to get the truck. When he left, Mother pointed to the kitchen chair and said that we should kneel and pray for a safe and successful journey. By the time Dad returned with the truck, we were ready to go.

We had travelled about two miles on our trip, when Mother discovered that she had forgotten her dentures. Dad was not a happy person. We turned around and got the dentures. I have wondered many times since how many people would have remembered the dentures, but forgotten to pray.

We got to Rochester. Little David prayed for Dad. As soon as the service was over, we headed back towards home. Although Dad's headaches did not go completely away, he said that the pain was not nearly as severe.

An interesting side story about our trip was that Dad spoke to his mother-In-law, my Grandmother Boden, that she should go on this journey. My grandmother was legally blind. Grandmother's reply was that if God wished to heal her, He could do it in her home. My grandmother died blind.

It was much later in life that Cathy and I went to a Benny Hinn meeting in Owen Sound. We had attended a number of his meetings earlier, as we appreciated his service. At the meeting in Owen Sound, there was a call for people with back problems to come forward for healing. My wife had a severe back problem. She had been to a number of physicians for help with no success. She went forward that night. She was prayed for. She was slain in the spirit and ended up on the floor. She was not pushed. She was literally slain in the spirit. That was over forty years ago. She has never had any back problems since that night. God does heal through physicians, but He also heals through prayer.

After I had my knee operation in 1976, the knee would not bend as it was supposed to. A number of different people prayed for my knee. I believed then that it was healed and I believe today that it was. It has never bent as it should, even after I had a knee replacement twenty years later. However - and this is a very big however - there has never been any pain. When the excellent doctor replaced the knee joint, he stated that it was full of arthritis. There has never been any pain, except for one brief time when I spent a couple of months in England to see our son Jamie playing hockey. After I returned from England, I spent a couple of months in Arizona. The pain disappeared, never to return. That was over twenty years ago.

Yes, the knee was healed of all pain, although the awkwardness of it remains.

——— LETTERS FROM RON ———

It was January 1976, when I went to the Markdale hospital to have the cartilage fixed in my left knee. When I woke up following the operation, I found that I was in a cast from my ankle to my hip. When the doctor began the operation, he discovered that my kneecap was completely in pieces. Without consulting my wife (since I was asleep), the doctor decided to save me another operation. He removed the kneecap.

I was to be in the cast for six weeks. At the end of that time, I was supposed to be fine, but I wasn't. After six weeks in the cast, my leg would only partially bend. I went through therapy, but it still would not bend. In August of that year, the doctor decided to take me into the hospital, anesthetize me, and while I was anesthetized, bend my knee. I was overjoyed when I woke up, because I was expecting to be in pain. There was none and with good reason. The doctor decided that if he bent the knee, he might tear something. As a result, nothing had been done to the knee.

During the next number of years, I carried on with regular activity. I played intramurals at the school, until I retired in 1994. My participation was limited to a degree, but I could always be a part of the team.

Before I had the operation, I had a lot of pain in my leg. Since the operation, I have not had any pain. There are those people who look at me, as I get up and down from my chair, or see me walking with my walker, thinking I am in pain. I am not.

When my knee was replaced in 2001, after my hip was replaced in 1999, the doctor stated that each one was full of arthritis, but there has been no pain, or even discomfort. There is a lot of awkwardness.

Why no pain? This leads into an interesting story. Shortly after the kneecap was removed in 1976, I attended a Christian Business Men's breakfast in Orangeville. My knee was prayed for. I believed it was healed. Is it possible that God in His wisdom healed the knee of all pain, but left me without full use of the leg? We do know that God works in mysterious ways. His wonders to perform.

I do know that, unlike my wife, I have never been "slain in the spirit". She was when her back was completely healed. I do know that we are able to travel by car, even to this day, because my wife is blessed with her health and the desire to drive. I have not had a license for the last six years, because the government of Ontario, in its wisdom, took away my privileges for a slight disability.

I do know that I do not have any pain, or even discomfort. I really do believe on that day back in 1976, God healed my pain. I accept His reason for handling my healing in this manner, even though I have no understanding of what happened, or why.

———— LETTERS FROM RON ————

It is now late in February. The resolutions of January 1st have, in many cases, been long forgotten. This is a process that takes place annually.

For many years now, my one resolution has been to serve my God better this year, than last year. The resolution is that my faith and trust in Jesus, as well as the Holy Spirit, will continue to grow as the year progresses. There were many days in the year that this happened, but there are other days that were "rocky", to say the least.

At the start of the new year, we wrote about a statement that the late Billy Graham made toward the end of his life. Mr. Graham's statement was that it is our job as humans to love one another, in spite of our differences. It is the Holy Spirit's responsibility to convict individuals and God the Father's responsibility to judge each human.

From the time in mid-2018 that we first heard this statement and the present time, there has been a real attempt by me to apply this to my life. It is not easy.

When the year 2019 began, it was decided that my resolution for the new year would be the fulfillment of Mr. Graham's statement.

This has led to at least thinking of Mr. Graham's statement once a day.

It is my job - your job - to love each and every person. There are no exceptions. Love takes many different forms. When we are travelling by plane, it is necessary for me to use a wheelchair. I would be foolish not to. It is a great benefit. Someone from the airport is responsible for pushing my wheelchair. Some of these individuals work long hours. Their pay is not great. We hope that the tip we give this person is at least sufficient. It is important to talk with this person and for a brief time, become part of that person's life. The life of the wheelchair pusher must, for a moment, become part of my life, the individual helped most by the wheelchair assistant.

And then there is the world of politics. How is it possible for us to love an individual whose political views are completely opposite ours? How can we love an individual we may feel is destroying our country, or would destroy our country upon coming to power? Mr. Graham says it is our job to love each and every politician, although we might never consider voting for that individual.

And of course, we need to love each and every member of our family. There are no exceptions. It is our responsibility. But none of this is easy.

CHAPTER 12

"THE EFFECTUAL FERVENT PRAYERS OF A RIGHTEOUS PERSON"

The heading of this chapter is a reference from the Book of James. The reference goes on to say that the prayer of a righteous person will have great results.

My mother did not leave her home very often, except for family events. She never attended any sporting event in which I was the coach. It was not that she was not interested. In fact, she wanted to know the time of the event and who we were competing against. She also wanted a report of the result of the game. Mother also wanted to know the day and hour of all my exams at school. She wrote the time and date on her calendar, so that during the time of the game, or exam, she could be praying.

There was the time that our team was playing a peewee hockey game in the Little N.H.L. for the rural Ontario championship. If we won this game, we would be going to Huntsville two weeks later as the representative of rural Ontario and compete for the provincial championship. This would be the weekend before my week of final exams at University. I told Mother about our game. I did not tell her that our games in Huntsville would be the weekend before my exams.

I was afraid that she might not want to pray for our team. In the semi-final game, we defeated a team that was much stronger than the Burks Falls team we were playing in the championship game. After two periods, we were ahead 3 to 1. We had the game well under control. Early in the third period, our goaltender, Jimmy Rutherford, got cut by the puck just above the eye. This was back in the days before goaltenders wore a mask. After going to the dressing room and getting Jimmy's bleeding stopped, the swelling began. It was decided that we were a better team having Jimmy in goal with only one good eye, than with our other goaltender with both his eyes. Jimmy's parents were in the dressing room and they agreed with the decision.

When the game resumed, our team received three penalties in a row. They were not violent penalties, but they were certainly deserved penalties. Burks Falls scored on each penalty. We lost the game and the championships 4 -3.

When I got home that Saturday night, I told Mom the result. I also confessed about the exams and that I had not told her earlier, because I wanted her to pray. Mother immediately replied that although she didn't know, God did.

Cathy and I had been married for five years. We were expecting our first child. When we told my mother, she immediately stated that the time to begin praying for the expected child was now. We immediately began following her advice. We carried on with the almost daily prayers after our son Jamie was born. I began going to his bed, placing one hand on his forehead and praying for him. Later, when his brother and sister were born, I followed the same process. I continued regular prayer for each of our children until they left home for new adventures in life.

It was not long until I began my regime of praying over a picture of each of them. I touch the picture and pray for the child in the picture. It has been many years since I began this form of prayer. There are now fourteen grandbabies. I now regularly pray for each of them, as well as their dad and mom, as I touch their pictures.

My mother's advice and example has never left me.

CHAPTER 13

ALL SUNSHINE MAKES A DESERT

Spring in Arizona often means weeklong periods will go by without rain. In fact, there are no clouds. The Phoenix area of Arizona is known as the Valley of the Sun. It is also a desert. Although this desert area has its own beauty, it is still a desert. In order to grow almost anything, moisture is needed, either by rain or irrigation. When there is a day of rain, there are always those people who wish it came another day. It is like the rain in our lives. Although it is needed for growth, we wish for it some other time. Maybe not at all.

As I was growing up, our family was a good community family. We certainly had the respect of a number of community people, but we were never part of the village's "in" crowd. This was not a problem for us. It was certainly not a problem for me. Each of us did our best. Dad served on the village council, the girls sang in the church choir and helped out with Sunday School. Dad was active in many church events. God was our strength.

I have already mentioned getting the strap in grade two. As a ten year old, I believed I should not have received it. I began attending Trail Rangers at Beeton's St. Andrew's Presbyterian Church. This was a very interesting experience. There was one family strongly supporting this church whose son stated that he would not be attending this group, if meetings were held in our United Church. I was becoming aware of the problems of denominationalism. Mankind, knowing so very little and seemingly understanding even less, divided itself into denominations, based upon interpretation of scriptures.

The problem that this boy was concerned about was a denominational split that had happened a number of years before our generation had even been born.

This boy was a friend of ours. A number of us had been invited to and attended his birthday parties, but he refused to enter our church, even though we were willing to attend his. There was rain happening. In the passing years, we have become much more aware of the problems of denominationalism.

While a member of Trail Rangers, I became its elected secretary and then the next year, I was elected president. The following year, I ran again for president. Another boy who attended St. Andrews finished tied with me in the vote. The minister of the church cast the winning vote for the other boy, stating as his reason, I had already served as president. Thus, the other boy should become the new president. Whether you agree with the minister's vote or not, it did result in some rain falling on this boy.

When I entered grade nine, I was nominated by my class as the male student representative to the Athletic Society. All students in the class had a vote, even though the girls had their own rep. I received the majority of the boys' votes. However, another boy in the class, a female charmer, got the majority of the girls' votes. When all votes were tallied, he became the representative.

In grade ten, I was nominated to be our class Student Council Rep. I lost the election. When I got to grade twelve, I was one of seven nominated for the Student Council Executive. Four would be elected. I finished last. However, there were some interesting stories that went with the election, all of which I enjoyed. In my large homeroom of almost forty students, I received the most votes of any candidate. This was very pleasing.

However, after the room election's votes were announced, I was in the hallway and I heard a boy from my home room, very much a member of the school's in-crowd, telling students from a different home room, "Can you believe that Pegg got the most votes in our room?" He himself clearly could not believe this.

On that same day, my brother had a friend confide to him, "I could not vote for your brother (me), because your brother would have Sunday School every day".

I was not bothered by the boy from the "in crowd" apparently surprised that I led the polls in our room. It was a little rain, but something that I had become used to. The Sunday School statement was not rain. I took it as a great witness of faith at work in my life.

The next year, which was to be my senior year, a friend of mine who was an inner circle member asked me to run again. He had been one of the four elected the previous year, but was not running. I said that I would run, if he would be my campaign manager. He agreed. I led the polls and as a result, became president of the council. During the school year, I also was president of our church young people's group, coached the village bantam hockey team, also played goal for our juvenile team - however did not pass all my subjects at school. As a result, it was back to school. As I only had to pass three courses to graduate, I again ran for student council and was re-elected president.

It would be almost twenty years later that I ran for the executive of Ontario Baseball and won. The following year, the appointed position of Secretary-Treasurer Registrar became available. The person holding this position was retiring after fifteen years.

From all my past experience, I did not wish to be at the yearly desire of the people. I knew that their desires often changed with no great reason for the change. I was one of three who applied. The other two were much more experienced than I. However, as Carmen Bush, the long-time member from Toronto stated to me after I had been appointed, I was the least experienced but the most wanted.

This was one of the greatest decisions of my life, as I served in this capacity for almost twenty years. Since I retired from the position, I have become one of three life members of Baseball Ontario and I am a member of its Hall of Fame.

Even more importantly, I became the person conducting prayer at the beginning of each meeting, including the annual meeting, during all of those twenty years. For a number of members of the executive, I became the person that they would come to talk with when they had a personal problem. In many ways, I was the unofficial padre of Baseball Ontario.

—— LETTERS FROM RON ——

Dr. Bob Jones was one of America's great evangelists and philosophers. One of his sayings was "Do Right"! He later expanded this saying to "Do right until the stars fall from heaven".

In his explanation of doing right, Dr. Bob stated that we should be so busy doing right, we won't have time to do wrong. Dr. Bob never stressed what the wrong was. He stressed only what is right. Each of us has this opportunity in our life. We need to be busy speaking with a clean tongue. We need to always be positive. We need to see the good in everything that happens to us. We need to praise our children. We need to eat sufficient amounts of good food. We need to eat in moderation. In fact, we need to do all things in moderation. We need to work. We need to rest. The list of good things that we can do just goes on and on.

We need to love our neighbours as ourselves. We need to give help, when help is needed. We need to leave our neighbour alone, when he or she does not want anything more than to relax in the comfort of their own home.

I am continuously amazed by the multitude - yes multitude - of people who help an elderly man with a walker. The world of travel is extremely kind to a person in a wheelchair. This I can say from personal experience. Many people go out of their way to offer help. It is amazing.

This is but one example of human kindness. These people are doing right.

I remember a man from my home village of Beeton who was in the local beverage room every night, except Sunday. Of course, in those days the beverage room was not open on the Sabbath.

This middle-aged man was also one of the village firefighters. I had watched him on the roof of a burning house leading the way to put out the fire. In helping his neighbour, he was a wonderful man. He often put his life in danger, leading the way in fighting fires. The equipment employed in those days was quite primitive, as compared with today.

This man always did right when it came to his neighbour, but he didn't do right in his own life. In his case, he probably died twenty years younger than he should have. He also had at least one early middle-aged offspring die, with alcoholism cited as a major factor.. This son had the potential to play in the NHL, but he never came close to reaching this potential. Why? Because he was too busy doing wrong to do right.

Most of us face conflicting times in our lives. It is not always easy to do right, but it certainly is an objective worth achieving.

CHAPTER 14

UNIVERSITY YEARS – BOB JONES

When we were passing from grade eight into grade nine, we were given a form to fill out. One of the things we were asked to write was what we planned to do after graduating from school. The form asked us to list our first, second and third choice. There was no question what my first choice was. I knew that I was going to be a minister in God's Church. There were those people who saw me as a little minister who was growing up to be an adult minister. My second choice was to be a Royal Canadian Mounted Police officer. The third choice was one Canadian boys still dream of. It was to be an N.H.L hockey player.

In reality, the second and third choices didn't matter. I was going to be a minister. My mother was very happy. I had already become a great follower of the young Billy Graham. When I read that Mr. Graham had attended Bob Jones University in Greenville, South Carolina, I began to research that University. The more I researched it, the more excited I became. When I discovered that an instrumental music ensemble from Bob Jones was coming to the Avenue Road Church in Toronto, my brother and I drove to Toronto to hear this group. I was more impressed than ever. Dr. Bob Jones Senior, the founder of the University was a good friend of Mother's radio pastor, Clinton Churchill. Bob Jones was also a great friend of Oswald J. Smith, founder of the Peoples Church in Toronto. In fact, Oswald J. Smith's son, by this time the pastor at Peoples Church, was a graduate of Bob Jones.

It seemed that everything added up. With Mom and Dad's blessing, I applied and was accepted. When I needed an extra year to complete my high school, the application was put off for a year, but I was still headed to Bob Jones.

When I arrived on the campus of the University, I felt that I was in a place closer to Heaven than I had ever been. Dr. Bob spoke the first night that I was there. This was in the fall of 1957. Dr. Bob spoke on the need for revival in North America. It was such a powerful message, that I would have gone on a crusade with Dr. Bob the next day, if he would have asked.

The quality of the music productions at the school, along with the acting that went with them, was unbelievable to this young Canadian boy.

It was not long, however, before this Heavenly place began to raise some question marks in my mind. Each day we were blessed to hear the top ministers in America, as they came to speak at morning chapel, at which our attendance was compulsory. Following morning chapel was lunch. Quite often the main subject at lunch was the speaker at the morning chapel. The discussion could become quite critical over some statement that the speaker had made. It's important to remember that the speakers were among the elite Christian speakers in America. I began to get the impression that the University could not be wrong.

It was during the early months of the fall when I became aware that Billy Graham only stayed at Bob Jones for one semester, before he transferred to a school in Chicago.

There were two sittings for each meal. The second meal at supper was primarily for those who played intramural sports. I played in goal for our team's soccer squad. One evening as we were walking to supper, I stated that I hoped that we were not going to have chili for supper (their chili was very spicy). One of the senior boys who was walking with our group, said I should be careful about making such a comment. He said it could be considered as a criticism of the University. This senior's statement really rang a bell with me. I began thinking is this the type of place that I want moulding me?

As the weeks and months reached towards Christmas, I found myself in a very conflicted state.

I loved the University. I do to this day. I loved the music, the special programs and the preaching. My faith grew during my time at the University, but I was not really happy. I was also beginning to question my call to the ministry. I loved it when I went out with a group of fellow preacher boys on a Saturday, or Sunday to preach the gospel. I probably could write a short book even today about the amazing and exciting experiences I had, but I was no longer sure that God had called me to be a minister. I began to seriously wonder if my call was to please the people who said I should be a minister, instead of the call of God.

When I came home at Christmas, I had every intention of going back. However, I became involved in a one-sided conversation with a fellow student in the back seat of the car that was taking us both to Cleveland. When this young man discovered that I planned to go to the high school dance when I got home, he was more than appalled. He continued to lecture me for hours on how wrong this was.

He was lecturing me about going to a dance at the school where I had been head boy for two years and had been part of the committee that was in charge of every school dance. I had used these dances as a chance to talk about the gospel of Jesus Christ. A school dance was very much a part of my mission field. This is the way I had always lived my life.

In short, I went to the dance as part of my mission field, but I did not return to Bob Jones University.

In spite of this, Bob Jones is very much a part of who I am today.

——— Letters from Ron ———

After one of his crusade meetings many years ago, Billy Graham was approached by one of the people who had attended. This person said to Mr. Graham that he (she) did not like Billy Graham's methods.

Billy then asked the person what was his (her) method. The person replied that he (she) did not have a method. Mr. Graham stated that he still liked his own method better.

When the Graham team was starting to conduct their second crusade in London in the late 1950s, some of the new young reporters for the papers stated in an editorial that it was the emotion caused by the singing of "Just As I Am" that caused the people to come forward. Mr. Graham knew that this wasn't true. He knew that it was the power of the Holy Spirit.

However, because of the reporter's comments Mr. Graham made the decision to have no music at the time of the altar call. The altar call was given. On the first night without music, there was a slight hesitation. The people then got up out of their seats and came forward in the same numbers that they always did. This went on for a couple of weeks. At this time, the reporter asked the Billy Graham team to begin leading in the singing of Just As I Am. The journalist said that the silence was killing him (her).

For me, I have always been amazed to see the hundreds and thousands who have come forward at each meeting. It seems that the people have literally poured out of their seats. Although there is no question that a number of those people who came forward never saw their faith grow. It is astounding to hear the testimony of many more that through the years have an amazing testimony of faith.

We also had the great opportunity of attending the Phoenix First Assembly of God church in Arizona for many years. The Pastor was Pastor Tommy Barnett. Like Billy Graham, when Pastor Tommy gave the alter call at the conclusion of the service, the people literally poured out of the seats to accept Jesus as Lord and Saviour. This happened Sunday after Sunday. One of the reasons it happened was because each Sunday, the church had many buses that went out about the city. The passengers riding these buses changed each Sunday.

As with Billy Graham, Tommy relied on the Holy Spirit. There was also a large prayer group who met in the church each Monday morning at six o'clock for the purpose of praying for continuous revival.

Billy Graham also believed in the importance of prayer. Each and every one of his crusades had many prayer groups meeting well before the actual crusade.

In our Grey County today, there is a desperate need for revival.

The sincere prayer of His people will allow the Holy Spirit to move with might and power. Revival will happen.

CHAPTER 15

THE MONTHS AFTER BOB JONES
A TIME OF COMPLETE CONFUSION

My Dad's last words to me as I got in the car that would take me to South Carolina were, "Well son, we have searched out this University. We are satisfied that you are going there, but if it doesn't work out, there is always home." That was my Dad.

And so, it had not worked out. What should I do now? Dad had sold his grocery store and the business while I was at Bob Jones. He was winding down the bakeshop business. He did not need a baker. I did help with the baking business, but there was no future in that. I was soon helping in the Sunday School. I began coaching the bantam hockey team in need of a coach. I also became Ken Kelly's assistant coach on my brother's juvenile hockey team. Ken was still playing senior hockey. On a night, when the juveniles were playing and the senior team was also playing, I became the juvenile coach.

The minister at St. Andrew's Presbyterian Church, Reverend Taylor, was a very good friend of mine. He was the minister of the Beeton, Tottenham and Schomberg charge. He was also the supervisor of the charge to the east of Beeton that included Bradford, the Scotch Settlement and Coulson's Hill.

I became almost like his assistant. I usually was speaking on the Bradford charge, but when communion needed to be administered on that charge, Rev. Taylor took those services and I took the services at the Beeton charge.

In late February, I had an interesting experience. It was a Saturday night and the Beeton Juveniles were playing on the edge of Northern Ontario against Powassan. The senior team was playing at home. I was already committed to speaking at the Beeton charge on Sunday morning. Ken lent me his car to not only coach the team, but to transport a load of players.

It was a warm winter's day. The Powassan ice was natural ice. It was too soft to begin the game before nine thirty at night. The game, which we won, ended just before midnight. One of the cars that was with our team developed problems around Huntsville. We were able to find an all-night garage and get the car fixed. As we approached Orillia, we found ourselves in a snowstorm. It was after six-thirty on Sunday morning that I arrived home. The first service was in Beeton at nine-thirty. I told my mother, who was awake when I arrived home, that I was going for a short sleep, asking her to wake me up shortly after eight. I spoke in Beeton and Tottenham before lunch. I went home for another hour of sleep, before I went to speak in Schomberg at two in the afternoon. By God's grace, we made it.

By the way, Reverend Taylor gave me several books with sermons of various ministers that he had in his library. One of these books was D.L. Moody the great evangelist from Chicago.

When our granddaughter Aly turned nine, I gave her the Moody book.

CHAPTER 16

"BUT WHAT AM I GOING TO DO?"

Reverend Gardiner, our Minister in Beeton, thought that I should go to Presbytery and seek to become an official candidate for the United Church ministry. I went along with the idea. Reverend Jim Shilton from Alliston was in charge of the committee. After I fielded a number of questions, Reverend Shilton and the committee concluded that I was not ready to become a candidate. It was suggested that I could go to Northern Ontario as a lay supply minister for a rural charge needing a minister. I agreed to this.

By the way, even though our beliefs were quite different, Reverend Shilton and I eventually became very good friends. He was a bit of liberal while I was - and am - a strong Conservative. Rev. Shilton performed our marriage and he baptized all three of our children. He came to Flesherton after he had retired for health reasons to baptize our youngest, Stacey.

As a result, I was heading to Cochrane to be the lay supply preacher on the "Clute – Island Falls" charge which had six different locations for me to minister to on different days of the month.

As I prepared to go to Cochrane, some interesting things happened in my life.

On the main street in Alliston, I met Fraser Rose who told me he was going to Waterloo College in the fall. I had never heard of this college. One of the reasons that I did not want to go back to school was I did not want to go to a big city like Toronto. Anyway, I was glad that Fraser was going to this small school.

Back in Beeton meanwhile, I was asked to supply teach at the public school for a couple of days. It was an enjoyable experience. Then as I passed by her home, I met this very fine woman, Miss Willowbee. She asked me how I was enjoying being a teacher.

She said she had spoken to the person who got the supply teachers. She said she hoped if I taught for a couple of days, I would become interested in teaching. I did not reply and was likely wise not to, because the singular thought in my mind was "Lady, I will NEVER become a teacher". It is very obvious that Miss Willowbee and all of her experience had a much greater insight than me.

On the last Sunday before I was to head north to Cochrane, I was speaking on the Bradford charge. Mr. Ritchie was the local druggist. He and his wife invited me to lunch. His daughter and boyfriend were also there. They were presently attending Waterloo College and suggested over lunch that I should consider going to that school. Again, I didn't reply, but in my mind, I "knew" that I was not going back to school.

The next Saturday morning, I was in our driveway preparing to drive the brand-new Volkswagen Dad had helped me purchase, up to Cochrane.

My Dad's final words were, "Well son, you are finally getting to do what you want to do." How could I tell him that this was not true?

CHAPTER 17

"CLUTE ISLAND FALLS"

It was an eight-hour trip to Cochrane. I made one stop to get gas. My Mother had made me a lunch to eat along the way. It was supper (dinner) time, when I arrived at the apartment of Alex and Ruth Taylor. They would be leaving, after the two services the next day. Their apartment was to be my home for the next year.

The Taylors were moving to Holstein, just outside of Mount Forest. Alex would be the student minister of a four-point charge. During the week, he was going to be attending Waterloo College to work on his Bachelor of Arts degree, on the road to becoming an ordained minister of the United Church. Yes, you read that correctly. He was going to be a student at Waterloo. It hit me like a ton of bricks. I had never even heard of this college a month ago. I was now having my third conversation about this school. This was very interesting. I was learning once again that God works in mysterious ways, His wonders to perform. He often uses other people to speak to each of us.

The other news that Alex shared with me was not nearly as exciting. A ten-year-old boy was going to the church camp near Timmins the next day. Alex had "volunteered me" to drive the eighty miles to the camp. I was not very impressed. I had just driven eight hours this day. I really did not need to drive close to another four hours the next day. Of course, I did not voice my feelings. After the two services were over on Sunday morning and the Taylors were on their way to Southern Ontario. I drove this young boy to the camp.

It was when we arrived at the camp, that one of the most unbelievable moments took place in my life. I helped the young man get registered and settled in. I became very aware of the excitement and noise of the camp.

I suddenly came alive!

For the first time in months there was an excitement within me. This was the very first time I became aware that "kids are my lifeblood". This is as true today, as it was that day at the camp. What an awesome God we serve.

As I was returning to my new home, it was quite a different person behind the wheel of the car, than had driven the eight hours the day before and who had driven four hours more to the camp. God showed me that I would only be on this charge for the months of June, July and August. I was going to return to school. I was going to Waterloo College to study to be a high school teacher. I would become a teacher at my former high school, Banting in Alliston. I would join teachers like Miss Bambrook, Mrs. Mary Coulter and Mr. Harold Pearson, who had spent their entire teaching careers in the Alliston area.

All the above happened. I went to Waterloo that fall. I became a teacher and taught at Banting in Alliston. However, God wasn't through speaking to me about my teaching career. After four years of teaching at Banting, I would go to Huron Heights in Newmarket. But, I am getting way ahead into my story.

The hardest job I had was telling all this to Dad. He was always one hundred percent supportive. It took me over two weeks to get around to telling Dad. He asked me a few questions and once again, was fully supportive of his eldest son.

I also had to inform the United Church that I was not staying beyond August. I had to get accepted as a student at the College. Yes, that young boy who entered grade nine knowing exactly what he was going to do, was NOT going to be a preacher. He was NOT going to be a Royal Canadian Mounted police officer. He certainly was NOT going to be an N.H.L hockey player. He was going to be a teacher.

Although I was not going to be a preacher, my faith certainly never waivered. My faith had grown very much. Jesus was the complete Lord of my life.

The words that kept repeating through my mind were trust and obey. As a result, I would not rust and decay.

—— LETTERS FROM RON ——

When Brian Clark passed away over twenty years ago, he left behind a little black box with instructions that it was to be opened upon his death.

One of the items in the box was a short story entitled "Table for Two". This short story was about Jesus sitting at a restaurant table, waiting for the person who had promised to meet Him there. Day after day, Jesus is there waiting, but the human never does come.

I was in Cochrane in Northern Ontario for three months in 1958 as a lay supply minister for the United Church. I was originally supposed to be there for a year. However, I decided to go back to University in Waterloo. The twelve months in the north became three.

During the first two months I was there, I was very busy doing the job of visiting homes and going for visits to the hospital. I had visited almost every home by the end of the two months. I did not enjoy this visiting. It was the result of these months that I came to realize that I was not really cut out to be a minister. I loved to preach and still do, but I found the visitation component, while important to a good pastoral minister, was not for me.

As a result of these two months of experience, I did not want to do any visitation unless it was completely necessary.

As a result, I was not very busy during this third month. I was overjoyed when my brother came to visit me on one of the weekends, then when three of my friends from home came to visit me for five days close to the end of August.

I remember crying my eyes out when they left. I only had one week left in Cochrane, but I was very lonely. It was by far the loneliest time that I can ever remember. For me, that month of August 1958 was a very long one.

In the early 1970s just shortly after we moved to Flesherton, I received the baptism of the Holy Spirit. I came to realize when I had accepted Jesus as a small boy, that Jesus, in the form of the Holy Spirit, came to live in me as is described in the gospel of John.

As a result of this realization, I have never been lonely since. Jesus is always with me. Although I may not have any human sitting at a table with me, I have Jesus in the form of the Holy Spirit always with me. He and I talk in a shared conversation. I am never alone. As a result, it is very difficult to be lonely.

I am always at the table for two with Him.

Yes, He is risen. He is risen indeed!

CHAPTER 18

LESSONS THAT WERE BEING LEARNED

I was not going to be a minister in a church serving a congregation but one of the things on which I had concluded is that being a Christian is a twenty-four hour a day, seven day a week life.

I loved preaching. I still do today. There is no thrill quite like it. God and I made an agreement when I left the ministry to go to school, that I would never keep one cent of what I was paid to preach, as long as I was not in full time professional ministry. Over sixty years later, this agreement still stands. I pay my travel expenses out of my own pocket.

During the three months that I was on the Clute – Island Falls charge, I spent the first month visiting everyone on the charge. This included a man living in a country cabin, who met me at his gate with a shotgun across his chest. On the other hand, I had many great visits with many wonderful people.

After I had visited all the people, the taste left in my mouth was not enjoying the visits. It wasn't the people. It was the process. As a result, I was soon doing very little visiting.

It was the same with hospital visits. I knew that this was very important. It is completely essential, but I did not look forward to this. In my own life I have visited many dying relatives and friends. This is no problem. This is not part of a job. It is part of my love for my family and friends.

In other words what I learned at Clute - Island Falls was that the only part of paid full-time ministry that I felt comfortable with was the actual preaching.

As mentioned earlier, I had discovered on my first afternoon on this job that kids are indeed my lifeblood.

There was another important lesson of life I had begun to realize - that other people, even people who only know you casually, have a clearer understanding of you (me), than you (I) do myself. It is not wise to set aside advice that someone gives to you without any consideration. In fact, it is wise to consider the advice at least a couple of times.

And so, it was off to school.

I was able to rent a shared room with the Morrison family just across the road from the College. Mrs. Morrison and her almost fifty year old daughter owned the home. It was a major blessing to have Mrs. Morrison, approaching her eightieth birthday, enter my life. She was a little Scottish woman no taller than five feet one inches and never quite weighing ninety pounds. Her deceased husband had been the treasurer of the largest Presbyterian church in Kitchener for over four decades. This little lady always had a smile.

I did not get to choose my roommate, although it turned out to be an old high school chum, Bob Mitchell. However, when the Morrisons discovered that he was in the co-op engineering program and not only had quite a different schedule to me, but the regular program, Bob was denied as a renter.

In truth, the Morrisons were not really in charge of their own room. Yet they were part of God's bigger plan. My new roommate, not planned by me at all, was the student minister from Holstein, Alex Taylor. This could only be arranged by God. This was the beginning of a lifelong friendship. To me it is still amazing that God arranged the roommates. It is even more amazing, because Holstein would become a significant part of my life in future years.

CHAPTER 19

WATERLOO COLLEGE

My dad and mom were behind their son one hundred percent. I had saved enough money to pay my tuition and buy my books. I didn't ask Dad for any. He told me he would give me twenty-five dollars every two weeks to help with my expenses. In truth, I had no other income. The cost for my room was thirteen dollars every two weeks. That left me with twelve dollars for food. I was driving a couple of students from my hometown, to the University of Guelph. Their small contribution paid for the gas. I went home every weekend to Beeton. My Mother sent me enough sandwiches to sustain me, until lunch on Wednesday. I would have them with a bowl of soup.

On the weekend in Beeton, I was teaching a young teenage Sunday School class. I was also working with the minor hockey house league at the arena on Saturday mornings. This was the beginning of Beeton Minor Hockey. Both the Sunday School class and the hockey were full of my lifeblood of young people. It is amazing to me as I look back, how important these two groups would be to me throughout my entire life.

Please don't try to tell me that I could have arranged this. Only the Holy Trinity could - and has.

On the first weekend that I was home from University, I went to the Teen Town dance at the arena in Alliston. Remember the boy from

Bob Jones who warned me that I should not go to the dance, when I was returning from my semester?

At Teen Town that evening, I was acting the part of the "big shot" home from college. Well, I had been president of the student council for two years. I wore my college initiation beanie. I danced with a number of young ladies who were present. My beanie went home with one of them, but there was another girl there that evening I wished had worn the beanie home.

When I returned to Teen Town a few weeks later, a mutual friend of this young lady and myself said to me as we danced, she knew of a young gal there who would like to dance with me. Having some idea of who it was, I took a shot at identifying her. I correctly described the girl. Catharine Mary Williams and I danced together that night. We went on a skating date in Bradford the next night. She was fifteen, in grade eleven and I was twenty-one, at University. As I write this book, we have been married for fifty-four years after a long and often interesting six years of courtship, including a two-and-a-half-year engagement.

On one of our earliest dates, I asked her if she was a Christian. She was a member of the United Church in Alliston. Her Mother had arranged for her to go to the Christian camp run by InterVarsity Christian Fellowship. At that camp, she had made a commitment of her life to Christ. By the way, the young lady who had worn the beanie home, had brought it back and it became part of Cathy's memories, as well as mine.

I had a schedule for school and the weekend. I worked very hard at the school from Monday morning to Friday afternoon. My books were left at school. They did not come home with me. I have never done one minute of schoolwork on a Sunday. That includes my time as a student and the thirty-four years that I taught. I have often got up at four o'clock on a Monday morning to study for an exam that I was going to have that day. I have always believed in seeking first the Kingdom of God and His righteousness - but I also am very human.

Each morning, Waterloo University College had a daily chapel. No classes were held for this half hour. A student had the choice of going to chapel, or going for coffee. I attended the chapel most days.

There were quite a variety of speakers at this Lutheran service. One morning a speaker from Niagara Falls had as his main theme, "the newspaper". He stated that you could find out how successful a person was going to be, by the way the person read the newspaper. If the person began at the front page and read through the paper, the person was going to be a success. I knew right then that I had no hope of success. I always began with the comics, then I read the sports pages and if I had any time left, I might read the front page. After hearing this man's presentation, I did not change my way of reading the paper. I would not give up my daily chuckle from Charlie Brown for almost any front page.

———— LETTERS FROM RON ————

One of my favourite hymns is the one that begins with the words, "...the Church's one foundation is Jesus Christ, her Lord". The Bible talks about a foundation built on a rock and one that is built on sand. The building built on the foundation of a rock will last. The building built on a foundation of sand will have a very short life span.

The foundation of Jesus Christ is one that believes that Jesus is the living Bible and that the Bible is the printed Jesus. It further believes that the literal Bible is the only correct interpretation of Jesus. Winston Churchill, the great World War II prime minister of England and also proven to be quite a scholar, stated that when all the facts are in and history is complete, we will see plainly that the literal Bible is correct.

It is true that historiography, which is the history of history, states that the facts of history are subject to change with new evidence. Many are examples of this. Winston Churchill has stated that new evidence will, in the end, verify the literal Bible.

And then there is the world of science. Many are the discussions and differences of opinion stated about science and the Bible. The people who have the foundation of the rock, Jesus Christ, believe that the Bible is scientifically correct. They would challenge those who say it isn't by simply stating that many of the findings of science are in a state of flux. In other words, the new findings continue to change what is accepted as the most recent fact in the world of science without the foundation of the literal Jesus.

In reality, it all comes down to the foundation.

As the old hymn goes on to say, Jesus came down from Heaven and shed His blood, so that each and every person can have life with Him in Heaven, when that person allows the literal living Jesus to become part of his, or her life.

A watered-down Jesus is not that rock. The more one waters Him down, the more the rock crumples into the sand.

CHAPTER 20

YEAR TWO AT WATERLOO

No one year in my life has had more significance than my second year at Waterloo. I had decided to try out for the college hockey team. This would be a major commitment. I went to the first practice and discovered from the drills that I was probably the third fastest skater amongst the players. This was very encouraging. Since I had played most of my minor hockey as a goalie, I had not developed my skills as a forward. It was for the position of forward that I was trying out. After three weeks of practice, I found myself on what appeared to be the third, or fourth line.

It was a Thursday afternoon. We were scheduled to play our first exhibition game that next Tuesday night. Before this game, there was a practice scheduled for Sunday morning, after which the game roster would be posted.

I could not attend the Sunday morning practice, as I was scheduled to speak that Sunday morning at Letterbreen Church at a special youth service. I had a previous agreement with my roommate Alex Taylor to take their special service in one of his churches some months before this time. I was to go to Alex and Ruth's home on Saturday night.

I explained my situation to the coach. He just said thanks for telling him.

I went to Letterbreen and spoke. They gave me fifteen dollars cash. After lunch, I headed back to Waterloo. As I travelled, I came to realize that I had two problems. I did not know if my name would be on the list of players for Tuesday's game. I also had a money problem. It was the money problem that dominated my thoughts, as I travelled.

The fifteen dollars I had received was three times the amount of money that I had in my wallet. On the other hand, I had an agreement with God that any money that I would receive would go directly back into His work. My thoughts wandered. One minute I was keeping the money. The next minute I was giving it to God. By the time I arrived in Waterloo, I had come to realize that I had to keep my agreement with God. The fifteen dollars was mailed to the National Bible Broadcast the next day.

The first place I went when I arrived in Waterloo was to the arena, to see if my name was on the list. It wasn't. I was not scheduled to play in the game on Tuesday.

On Tuesday morning, we got our results back from a Spanish test. Spanish was by far my most challenging subject. In my first year at the University I spent more time on Spanish than on all the rest of my subjects put together. I still only got a "C". We got the test back. I failed! This was, for me, a very major crisis. Why? It was because I could not let my dad and mom down. They had supported me when I returned from Bob Jones. They had supported me when I lasted only three months in Northern Ontario. For my Dad and Mother's sake, I could not fail.

I never did return to the arena. My hockey tryout was over. I cut myself from the team.

In reality this was one of the most important decisions in my life. If I had continued to play hockey at College, I would not have been able to go home on weekends. I would not have been able to teach my Sunday School class. At least three of these girls have gone on to play major roles in community efforts and in churches. These women have been lifelong friends. Two of them still play significant roles in my life.

I also would not have been able to coach and manage the Saturday morning hockey. Three boys out of this group went on to play N.H.L. hockey. Three others had great hockey careers at the University level.

Several others have been successful in other fields of work. The friendships with this group that continue to this day are numerous.

And then there is the Spanish. In my second year at Waterloo, the college was moving from being associated with Western, to becoming an independent school.

As they were still associated with Western, there was a day in February that we had no classes to go to. The professors went to Western that day to help set our final exam. I told my mother about that day, so that she could be praying for the Spanish Professors to set an exam I could pass. We both prayed that day. When I opened my exam in April, I immediately closed my eyes in a prayer of gratitude when I read the exam. The exam could not have been more to my liking. I still only got a "C", but I passed.

And then there was the young woman that I had met at Teen Town. Our relationship existed but it was spotty. I would have seen much less of her if I had been playing hockey. As it turned out, the boy's hockey tournament I was to coach in was in Alliston. She and her Mother were at the arena most of the day helping. We won this regional tournament. The provincial tournament was at Base Borden just a few miles from Cathy's home. She invited me to supper, after our Friday afternoon game. It was my first visit to her home. After supper, she returned with me to the Base Borden arena to watch more hockey. After the game, I took her home. As I was going down the lane from her house, it suddenly hit me that I was really in love with this girl.

All these things I have mentioned were based upon one decision. It was the decision to put God first. Amazing!! It truly is. If you look closely, you can see a lifetime very much wrapped up with this decision.

I am so glad that God gave me the problem of Spanish.

—— LETTERS FROM RON ——

It was the first Saturday in February. The Pittsburgh Penguins were in Toronto to play the Maple Leafs. I am a Penguins fan. I was more excited than I ordinarily get watching a regular season NHL game. The Penguins had been playing well in their up and down season. On the other side, I would get to see Travis Dermott playing against the Penguins. Travis is the grandson of a couple that I knew in high school. Travis is the son of Jimmy Dermott, who grew up in Tottenham. I had the privilege of coaching Jim as a peewee baseball player. Jim always was a gentleman, with a very positive temperament. He was also my nephew's best friend. In fact, our nephew, Steve Thompson was attending the game as the guest of Jimmy Dermott.

The game itself did not impress me as being exciting. At the end of the second period, Pittsburgh was ahead two to one. It looked like the Penguins were going to win. However, halfway through the third period, the Leafs scored. It wasn't just any Leaf. It was Travis Dermott who had tied the score. Travis also got an assist. A couple of minutes after Travis tied the score, the Leafs scored what would prove to be the game winning goal.

The first star of the game was Travis. I was full of joy for Travis, his mother, his father Jim, and his grandmother Ruth. Also my nephew Stephen, who was seeing Travis play live for the first time at the home of the Maple Leafs.

I am always a bit sad when the Penguins lose, but it wasn't like they were playing for the Stanley Cup. Besides, the Penguins had been up and down like a yo-yo all year. As I write this column a couple of weeks after the game was played, my joy for the Dermott family far outweighs any disappointment over the Penguins' loss.

It is a reminder that we need to always keep things in their proper perspective. It is really so much of what life is. As the old Arab saying goes, all sunshine makes a desert. Even more than that, much of life is grey. It is not black and white. Each of us needs to find the good in the events of life, even in a regular season NHL hockey game. We need to enjoy the moment. We need to love living.

It is rather interesting that since that game, some Toronto sports writers have been questioning Mike Babcock's handling of Travis this year, stating that the statistics indicate Travis deserves more ice time with a better partner than he usually has.

The grey area continues.

CHAPTER 21

AND THEN THERE WAS YEAR THREE – WATERLOO

Year three at Waterloo did not hold nearly the drama that year two held.

I continued to attend chapel as a daily event. In this final year at Waterloo, I became part of the committee that helped arrange the services. Along with Alex Taylor, I became very active in the InterVarsity Christian Fellowship. This third year, I became the president.

When the school's first ever winter carnival was taking place, I strongly encouraged our group to enter the ice sculpture event. We did. We built a duplicate of the school's crest, with a rotating cross in the middle. We won. It was a great witness, especially in the first year of what became a major campus event.

During the summer between my second and third year, I came to discover that I could apply for a small bursary from the Ontario government, because of the low income of our family. I applied for and received a grant of three hundred dollars. This would be comparable to a grant well over $3,000.00 today. I found out that I was getting the grant early in January. I had never before been in possession of this amount of money. My tuition was paid. My textbooks were paid for. I had no debts. Dad and Mom were still giving me twenty-five dollars every two weeks. I was still getting gas money from the boys that I brought back to Guelph.

I had the thought in my mind that maybe I should buy Cathy an engagement ring. This idea did not make a great deal of sense. I did not have a job. I was still in school. Cathy was in her last year of high school, with every intention of going to University. It was at this time that the silliness of this idea became completely evident. As I drove her home after a Friday night dance at the high school, Cathy told me she no longer wanted to go steady.

It was a couple of weeks after this that I was going back to school. I had let the boys in Guelph off at their University.

As I turned a corner at the edge of Guelph, something in the car went clunk. The transmission had fallen out of the Volkswagen. The bill to replace the transmission was two hundred and ninety-two dollars. My amazing God knew of my need, when I didn't even know there was a need on the horizon.

This was also the year that our peewee boys hockey team won the rural Ontario championship in Bradford. We would then go to the All Ontario Championships in Penetang and Midland. Two of the members of the team were our goalie Jimmy Rutherford and John Gould. John was our leading scorer and the heart of our team. As I write this book, Jimmy has just been elected to the one and only Hockey Hall of Fame.

Our Beeton bantam team had also won the rural championship. I had previously coached a number of these players. The one who stood out was a player named Wayne Carleton. Both the Montreal Canadiens and the Toronto Maple Leafs were seeking to sign Wayne. Another team at the bantam tournament was Parry Sound. The same scouts interested in Wayne were also very interested in another player named Bobby Orr. The two teams played. Bobby Orr and his Parry Sound team won an exciting game.

One of the scouts who was very interested in both players was none other than Scotty Bowman, the one and only.

Our peewees lost their first game in this All Ontario tournament, but we won the rest of our games and reached the Consolation championship game. We won the semi-final game at the Midland arena. We had to get to the Penetang arena for the championship game. It happened that Scotty Bowman was travelling from the Midland arena, to the one in Penetang. He took a carload of the Beeton players.

We won the Ontario Consolation Championship.

I am so glad that our God puts some big bumps in our pathways. I am overjoyed that one of my bumps was the subject of Spanish, as I have previously mentioned.

There is one other sidelight about this team that needs to be mentioned. He really is much more than a sidelight.

His name is Clare "Butch" Holmes. In this championship game Butch got the first major penalty for fighting in the history of the "Little N.H.L." This was a sign of the hectic life this little guy would go on to live. He was a great little athlete, who hated practice. There were many times that I sent him home from practice, because he was just being a nuisance. However, I knew when it became gametime, he would give one hundred percent.

Butch's father was a veterinarian. Young Butch would soon follow his father into this vocation. Over my thirty-four year teaching career, he was one of just three people to whom I awarded the mark of one hundred percent for a major exam. On another occasion, I was supervising a school dance, to which his father had to be called, because Butch was drunk.

After he became a vet, Butch often got into problems entertaining unorthodox methods for treating animals. He also continued to abuse his body with chemicals.

Dr. Clare Holmes and I had a number of conversations throughout the years. None was more significant than the night he and I walked the streets of Atlanta, following John Gould's wedding. We spent the night talking about God. The two of us had a mutual admiration for one another.

He died young. He attended his Anglican Church on a regular basis. The demons in this world caused Butch not to achieve what he was so capable of. On the other hand, from what I know about Doctor Clare Holmes, I will be disappointed if I don't get to talk with him when I get to Heaven.

Thank you, my Dear Heavenly Father, my precious Jesus and beloved Holy Spirit, that I was not prepared to disappoint my dad and mom for the third time. Yes, the Spanish bump has been a great blessing to my life.

—— LETTERS FROM RON ——

When I attended University as a student, I lived in a private home with three students who rented a room. The home was less than a half a block from Waterloo University College.

The family renting out these rooms were the Morrisons. It was a bungalow. We three students had our room on the main floor. Mrs. Morrison and her daughter Grace slept in the finished basement. Mrs. Morrison was a Scottish woman who was approaching her eightieth birthday. Grace worked at an office job in Waterloo. Mrs. Morrison looked after the home.

Mrs. Morrison probably didn't reach the weight of ninety pounds soaking wet. She was always very cheerful and always had a smile on her face. Whenever a snowfall came, she cleaned her own sidewalk. One early January while doing this, she slipped and broke her collarbone. This did not take away her cheerfulness. She and I often had great conversations either standing in the kitchen or sitting in their living room.

In late January of my second year, Mrs. Morrison became very sick. We did not see her for over a month. We wondered if we would ever see her again. In late March, she was in her kitchen once again. On the second day, she was back upstairs and heading out the door, as I came home from classes. She had just finished doing her own dishes and told me she was going across the street to a neighbour's house. This neighbour family had just been blessed with a new baby. Smiling as we passed, she said that she was going out to help the new mother by washing her dishes and cleaning up her kitchen.

Wow!! She was eighty years of age. She had been sick. She was going to help a young neighbour one day after she was herself declared healthy enough to venture upstairs in her home, after being bedridden for well over a month!

She had me thinking of the song that we had sung in Sunday School as small children, "Jesus bids us shine with a pure clear light, like a little candle burning in the night. He looks down from Heaven to see us shine, You in your small corner and I in mine."

Mrs. Morrison was certainly shining in her corner. She always did. It is a reminder to each of us to let our candle shine in the service for Jesus. By doing this, each of us can help brighten this world.

CHAPTER 22

SUMMER TIMES

During the first half of my summer of University, I worked for the County of Simcoe road crew. Mr. George Whiteside was my boss. For the rest of the summer, I worked for Bill Dorsey picking potatoes. Over my last two summers, I worked on sod for Mr. John Verbeek. Mr. Verbeek was a fantastic Canadian born in Holland. Going behind the cutting machine, my job was to be on my knees rolling sod. I also had to load one sod at a time onto the sod trucks. It was the hardest physical work I have ever done. I had muscles that were still sore by summer's end.

My purpose for working in the summer was to make enough money to pay for my tuition and books upon returning to school.

Beginning the summer of 1958, I was invited to speak at the United Church in Cookstown to supply for their holidaying minister. This was the beginning of twenty-four consecutive years when I was speaking in Cookstown from one to five and six Sundays. Every cent of the money that the church paid me was given back to the church. Having said this, I was certainly blessed to partake of delicious meals regularly received in the home of Mr. and Mrs. Albert Kell. Their three children. Wilson, Allen and Irene Kell, are but three of the young Cookstown people who have become lifelong friends. The fact that I also taught many of the young people at Banting helped me further develop these contacts.

Two other young people that immediately come to mind are Marilyn Glass and Frances Mae Hindle Balodis. Frances is a genius in her own right teaching piano. Frances also plays the church organ and has been the conductor of a number of choirs. Marilyn has become a very good friend.

Summer was also baseball. Who could possibly have guessed that when Bob and Aimee Rutledge quit coaching the Juvenile team, Bob (a key to my hockey coaching involvement) would ask me to manage the team? For me, this would also be the beginning of over sixty years (present time) of working in baseball in the province of Ontario. It was not many years before I became president of the juvenile league.

Baseball also led to a number of interesting nights on the main street of Beeton. Two of the young men who played on this team, spent hours and hours with me afterward just talking. I would soon be providing them with rides to the University of Guelph.

The one young lad was our best pitcher and one of our leading hitters. He was also an outstanding student, who was going to University to study to be a vet. The other boy had just begun ball a couple of years before this. He was still in the early part of a fledgling ball career. I also taught his two sisters in our Sunday School. This young man was a genius in math. He received a complete math scholarship to the University of Guelph.

Most of our discussions were on the subject of Jesus. Neither of these two young men were willing to give their life to Jesus. Neither was convinced by any of our many discussions to even consider a life that would be lived for Jesus.

There is no question that I was academically the weakest student of the three.

The pitcher went to school and became a vet. He was virtually given the practice of a very successful vet who was retiring. This man married a fine young woman and became interested in horses. This interest led him to betting on horses. He was not successful. He ended up losing his practice. While still under the age of forty, he died of a massive heart attack in his car on his way home from the track.

The other boy was blessed with a very fine Christian mother. He was the cleverest of us three boys. He went with his wife to one of the islands in the Pacific doing post graduate work. I had the honour of being the master of ceremonies at their wedding reception. His new wife was a great young woman.

She described to me what was happening on the island. They began to go to parties after work. Then they began to go to parties after the party, and then they began to go to the parties after the party after the party. He became an alcoholic. They separated. He had no stability. He was involved in a major car accident, suffering a brain injury and although he quit drinking, he was never the same again.

Let me repeat. There were three boys from Beeton. Two were outstanding students. One was slightly above average. The two outstanding students had many chances to accept Jesus as Lord and Saviour in this life, but never did. The poorer student of the three had been following Jesus since he was a little boy.

Thoughts of these summer nights bring nothing but sadness to this old guy. These nights were a learning time in his faith.

CHAPTER 23

THE TEACHING YEARS AT BANTING

One of the great things that happened at Banting involved the young people from Beeton. Most of the young people I had been involved with through hockey, baseball and Sunday School were students at Banting. Most people in Beeton knew me as Ronnie. All of these young people called me Ronnie. However, when I became their teacher, they all called me Mr. Pegg. There were only two times when a student called me Ronnie. On both occasions, the students immediately corrected themselves.

After I finished teaching at Banting, all of these young people reverted to calling me Ronnie.

My principal at Banting was Mr. Sid Owens. He wore his Christian faith on his sleeve. At the annual Christmas assembly, he was part of a male quartet of teachers who sang "Go Tell It on the Mountain." When I had the opportunity of speaking at the St. Johns United Church in Alliston, Mr. Owens conducted the service.

On top of his Christian faith, he was an excellent administrator. I have nothing but admiration for this man and his ability to lead people.

He asked me to be the teacher sponsor of the Inter-School Christian Fellowship group. This was the beginning of over thirty years of being the teacher sponsor.

One of the students in my first home room class was Wayne Wardell. He had many problems. When a special needs class was established for grade nine students a month after school opened, I was overjoyed that Wayne became a member of that class.

It was two years later when, as school was beginning, I was in a classroom waiting for the students to come to the Inter-School Christian Fellowship Meeting. Wayne walked into the room and took a seat at the back. I thought he must have made a mistake, thinking this was the detention room. Wayne had not made a mistake. He had become a Christian. He also became a member of my Grade 11 advanced history class. This boy who had been in a special needs class was now in an advanced class.

I will never forget the meeting at the end of the year when individual students were discussed. When Wayne's name came up and that he had passed all of his subjects as an advanced student, with marks over seventy ("B" average or better), one of the teachers asked "...wasn't this a boy who was in a special needs class"? Mr. Doug Nesbitt, a teacher also known for his faith, responded, "This young man had accepted Jesus as his Saviour". Wayne was now a new person.

After Wayne finished high school, he went on to become an ordained minister.

I began attending a prayer group at Mrs. Murphy's home. Ken Inkster and Doug Nesbitt, teachers from Banting, had been attending this group for some time. Mrs. Symons, the Anglican rector's wife, was also a regular member. The prayers of the group were primarily for revival in the area and particularly among the young people.

A ladies' group in Beeton which included Mrs. Hazel McCague and Mrs. Helen Dale, was also praying for a revival amongst the young people.

We had been in contact with Stan Izon, who conducted revival meetings for younger people. He came to St. Johns in Alliston on a Friday night for a rally. The church was almost full. It was decided to invite Mr. Izon back for an all-day outreach meeting in Beeton at Trinity United in the late spring. We established a youth committee to lead in the organization of this event. I began to meet with a half dozen young people. They had never been in a prayer group, but prayer became part of our meetings. Most of the group members struggled with this, but we did have prayer.

This meant that as we approached the Beeton meeting, there were three prayer groups actively praying for revival.

On the Saturday afternoon of the meeting, the church was full of young people involved with various activities. The women's group at the church prepared a great buffet dinner. After dinner, the church was packed with young people to hear Mr. Izon speak.

When the altar call was given, the seats in the church literally emptied as practically everyone in the church went to the altar seeking Salvation.

Mr. Izon had never had a meeting quite like this. The conclusion was that the prayer groups and the prayers were the key to the evening.

The need for more and more prayers was a growing theme in my life.

CHAPTER 24

THE NEWMARKET YEARS

In my final year as a teacher at Banting, I was the acting head of the history department. As the spring of that year approached, I was offered the headship at Huron Heights in Newmarket, where my future wife was teaching. There was no prospect of a job for Cathy in Alliston. The history head who had vacated his position was probably coming back. As a result, I accepted the job at Huron Heights.

The words God brought to me during the trip back to Cochrane, the Sunday afternoon I unwillingly took the young boy to camp, had concluded. I misunderstood the vision to include a lifetime of teaching at Banting. This was not to be.

At different times over the next thirty years of teaching, I attempted to return to Alliston, but this was not part of God's plan for us. Even after I retired and made attempts to move back to the Beeton–Alliston area, it was not God's will.

I was not receiving any long-range plans from God at this time. The only plan that He showed us was that we were going to Newmarket. This was an area that I was very familiar with, because Dad and Mom grew up in the nearby Mount Albert area. Our Pegg family had made many trips to Newmarket to shop, visit relatives, take my oldest sister Bernice to her heart specialist and to attend the Santa Claus Parade.

My new principal was Mr. Shepherd, a very fine Christian man. Huron Heights was only a couple of years old.

Mr. Shepherd asked me to begin an Inter-School Christian Fellowship group. During our six years at the school, the group never grew. It always had six or seven members. Most of this small group were members of solid Christian families. I did not understand why the group did not grow. A number of the teachers began a prayer group, but this prayer did not seem to have any effect upon the group.

It was only in the years following, when I received letters from some of the former members, that I came to understand the issue. These letters informed me that these students from Christian homes had only accepted Christ as their Saviour after they graduated from high school. In other words, the ISCF group had been important in these individuals becoming Christians. It took time for this to happen.

It is a great reminder of the words from Corinthians, that our job is to sow the seeds and that God, the Holy Spirit, will give the increases.

One of the members of the group who sent me a letter was Peggy Aldom. Peggy is the daughter of Mrs. Aldom, at the time a secretary in the school office. Peggy is the sister of Dave Aldom, who was a math teacher at the school. He was a member of our teacher's prayer group.

Mrs. Aldom was a great Christian warrior. I often went to the Aldom's Baptist church to speak. My wife and I usually returned to her mother's home in Alliston on the weekend. We went to the United Church, where she was dedicated and where we were married. At one stage, I volunteered to teach in the Sunday School in the United church in Newmarket. I never heard back, as the minister of the church at that time was not even sure that God existed.

On the other side in Newmarket, I often worked with the Newmarket ministerial committee. I had often felt the need to be baptized by immersion. This happened on a Sunday evening at the Baptist church on the main street while the organist played "He Touched Me." Working with the ministerial committee, we began to hold Friday night coffee houses at the Presbyterian church. We would have a Christian music group come to lead in an evening of praise. For one summer, we also ran a coffee house in an old automobile garage. This was open daily as a drop-in centre. A local family made a large donation in order that this ministry could take place.

All these events led to a Youth for Christ outreach ministry coming to town. Rev. Hepburn, the leader of the ministerial committee, asked me to approach the school to hold an assembly on the morning of the first day of the outreach. I approached Mr. Shepherd and he agreed. However, as the day was approaching, he began to have doubts. He even talked about cancelling the assembly. On the morning that he was to meet with me, I called my mother so that she could be praying as the meeting took place. Mrs. Aldom was aware of the meeting. As I passed her on the way to Mr. Shepherd's office, I asked her to be praying at her desk. After a good discussion, it was agreed that the assembly would take place.

As a result, many students from the school attended the coffee house downtown, where the outreach was taking place. If my memory is correct, over fifty young people accepted Jesus at the coffee house. Looking back from the year 2020, it would not be possible for this assembly at Huron Heights to even take place today. How times have changed!

While in Newmarket, I began pursuing my desire to be a principal. This included an interview with one of the school's superintendents. He was a regular attender at the Presbyterian church. In the course of the interview, I stated that until God wanted, I would never be a principal. No man could make me one. On the other hand, when God wanted me to be a principal, no man would stop me from being one.

I had no idea that God had something far different in mind for me, than becoming a school principal.

—— LETTERS FROM RON ——

I never got to know my father-in-law very well. He died of a massive heart attack, before my wife and I had been married a year.

Mr. Williams was a very prominent person in his community in Alliston. He served on the council for over a quarter of a century. Most of those years, he served as the town's Deputy Mayor. He was chair of the committee that built the new arena in the late 1940s. He played a significant role in attracting new industry to the town.

He was known as "Red" Williams, partially because of his red hair and partially because of his toughness and temper as an athlete. At one time, Mr. Williams was one of the best lacrosse players in Ontario. He played the sport until reaching his mid-forties. He was also an excellent baseball and hockey player. Our children are certainly blessed that both their grandfathers were excellent athletes. My own father played some pro soccer (football in his day, a hundred years ago). Each of the three was influenced by their grandfathers.

Mr. Williams was not a regular church attender. However, no harvesting or any activity like that took place on his farm and mink ranch on a Sunday.

It is very interesting to note that, although he was never a regular church attendee, three of the local ministers (including the area priest) came to his wake. Their visits were not casual visits. The three visited for the major part of an evening.

At the funeral home on the final morning of the open casket viewing prior to it being moved to the church for the service, I was in attendance at the funeral home. This just in case there were any late visitors.

I was the only family member present that morning. It was around eleven o'clock in the morning when a man came in who was not well groomed. He introduced himself. He lived at the edge of town in a shack behind an old mill which prepared food for animals. I was aware of his home.

He said he had to come and pay his respects to Mr. Williams. That Mr. Williams often helped him out with money from his own pocket.

In those few minutes, I discovered the most important lesson about my Father–in–law. Through the visiting hours, the funeral chapel had steady lines of people coming to pay tribute. The church would be full for his service. And yet, the most significant visit was by this man who, the morning of the funeral, had come to the chapel by himself.

CHAPTER 25

ON THE MOVE

Our first child was born in the spring of 1970. Jamie is his name. I was by now involved with coaching the Newmarket tyke baseball team. I also had become involved in the town's minor hockey system. Newmarket was beginning to grow rapidly. I was becoming restless.

I had no idea what kind of athlete that Jamie would be. I did know that in Newmarket, if you were not on the town's top hockey team, you probably would get one hour of ice time around six o'clock on a Saturday morning. In the village from which I came, we were often looking for another hockey player. Over thirty kids had tried out for the tyke ball team. In my former village, we would often be looking for a ninth player just to field a team. I wanted to give our child the same opportunity I had to participate.

As the spring of the year came, I became more and more restless. However, there were no jobs being advertised. I remember spending almost an entire Friday evening at a coffee house in the basement of the Presbyterian Church in Newmarket. Only God and I were present. I wanted Him to give me some answer that would relieve my restlessness.

One Friday at the end of April, one of my student teachers said that he was going to Flesherton the following day to interview for a job he had seen in the newspaper. After I finished talking to him, I picked up the paper and phoned for an interview. I was granted an interview on Saturday mid-afternoon.

I happened to be involved in an umpire clinic in Alliston Saturday morning. When the clinic was over, my wife and I headed to Flesherton. I was wearing a cardigan sweater. My wife said that I should have worn a sport jacket. I replied to her that if this job was to be, my sweater would be fine. By the way, she was wearing a cute green dress with white trim.

My student teacher was leaving the school in Flesherton, having completed his interview.

Mr. Bob Griffin, the school vice–principal and Gil LIttle, the head of the school's history department, were conducting the interview. Mr. Griffin began the interview by stating that this interview would be different. He immediately stated that over one hundred and forty applications had been received for this position, but this job was mine if I wanted it. He had been talking with our close friend, Huron Heights vice-principal, Mike Steele. He had also learned that I was heading seven teachers in a thriving history department.

As the interview continued, the principal Mr. Murray Juffs came in. He was wearing a cardigan sweater. We also discovered that the colours of the school were the very same green and white as my wife's dress.

When the interview was over, Mr. Little took us on a tour of the village and area, including the beautiful Beaver Valley.

As we left to return to Alliston, my mind was completely ablaze. I had just seen the fulfillment of a dream I'd had for years.

I knew that this was God's dream for us. However, my wife was not saying much about the prospect of moving to Flesherton. We went home and bounced the idea off Cathy's Mother, my dad and mom, and the seven-member history department, receiving a mixed reaction. There was also the fact that there would be no job for my wife. Flesherton would mean giving up her physical education headship as well as my history headship.

I had promised Mr. Juffs that I would call about the offer on Monday. By the way, Mr. Juffs stated to Mr. Little that I would not be taking the job. However, I called on Monday to ask for a two-day extension.

As Wednesday evening approached, I told Cathy I had to call Flesherton and give an answer. She was not saying much. I had to pick our cat up at the vet. As I left, I said that I had to call about the position when I came back. As I took the journey across town and back, I was in constant prayer. I knew we had to go. What would I do if she said no?

When I returned, I posed the question to her. Cathy said that it was up to me.

I said that I would be telling him that we were coming. While I talked to Mr. Juffs on the phone, my wife was crying at the kitchen table. Cathy's tears would be repeated numerous times, as we said our goodbyes to friends in the community and in school.

——— LETTERS FROM RON ———

We attended a Joyce Meyer convention in Phoenix. The church was full. There were two areas of overflow that were also full. Spokesperson Joyce was her usual inspiring self.

Joyce does not give the altar call at the end of her address. She has a man known as Pastor Mike. He comes out when Joyce is finished. Pastor Mike speaks for five minutes with his entire presentation being a call to those who have yet to accept Jesus as Lord and Saviour, to come forth and do so. Many responded. These people were given some literature to help them grow in their new faith.

No one describes the born-again experience from the early verses of John Chapter 3 better than Pastor Mike.

He states that when you accept Jesus into your life, it is like the driver of a car inviting Jesus to drive your car for life. You have been in the driver's seat. You slide over to the passenger side and hand Jesus the keys, putting Him in complete charge of your life.

The problem that many people have when they accept Jesus as their driver, they want to back seat drive.

A person wants to tell Jesus how He should drive your car of life. The person wants to give directions, but Jesus is the way. Each or us was created individually as a unique creature. God, the Creator knows exactly how each of us should operate. He understands completely the best way for each of us to go.

In the early 1990s I took three young basketball players to the Fellowship of Christian Athletes Camp, just outside of Gettysburg in Pennsylvania. The highway we travelled in Pennsylvania and New York State had many long hills. Our car began to heat up. I eventually felt that we needed help. I pulled into a gas station where the sign indicated that we could get mechanical help. I stated to the mechanic that, though I really know nothing about cars, I thought the carburetor was acting up. The mechanic informed me that this car did not have a carburetor. I did not have a clue that this change had taken place in cars. I had often heard my Dad, also not a mechanic, talk about carburetors.

Jesus is the ultimate mechanic. When we give Jesus the keys to our life, we need to leave those keys completely in His hands.

CHAPTER 26

THE FIRST YEARS IN FLESHERTON

One person that Gil Little introduced us to in Flesherton was Mrs. Geraldine Robinson. She was the wife of a local doctor and the one person most responsible for Grey Highlands Secondary School being built. She was interested in building houses in the village, to encourage teachers to live close to the school.

This was very exciting. I wanted to live in the village where my school was. My wife and I had explored the available housing. I am one of the world's worst handymen. The houses available all needed major work. We were not prepared to buy a house, because we were not 100% positive we would be staying.

Mrs. Robinson stated that she was prepared to rent the house to us for a year. If we decided to buy the house after a year, she would apply the rent money to our purchase price. She also worked with Cathy in deciding the house colours, the flooring and cupboards. The following spring, we purchased the home. This was just one of the many occasions that we would have the opportunity to work with Mrs. Robinson. It was also the beginning of an excellent relationship with my history head, Gil Little.

During my job interview, one question I recall Mr. Juffs asking was this. If I agreed to accept this job, who would be the head of the history department: Gil Little, or myself? I immediately replied that Mr. Little would be the head. This was the beginning of a seamless relationship between Mr. Little, Mr. Juffs and myself during the next couple of decades.

Within the first few months, my wife was teaching halftime at the school. After that time, neither of us had one moment of concern about having given up our past headships. Our friendships at Huron Heights did not fade away. We both retain close friendships with most we worked with in the Newmarket school departments.

For us both, the freedom of not being department heads allowed more freedom than ever to coach. Working with adults as the head of the department, was really not part of my lifeblood. Coaching kids and young people truly was. Cathy became a very successful volleyball coach at the school. God led me to witness dynasties in hockey and girls basketball.

The future of hockey in Flesherton did not look promising in the brand-new arena, as our little guys lost to the neighbouring town of Honeywood in their first league game sixteen to nothing. We never even had a shot on goal, but the dynasty did emerge. Under the leadership of others today, minor hockey is still providing championship teams almost thirty years after my retirement.

Our girls' basketball team won many district championships. Our junior girls team won eleven consecutive CWOSSA championships. There was a stretch when both the senior and junior girls won five consecutive double championships. Yours truly had the honour of coaching both teams through this entire dynasty.

But there was much more than this. As had my two previous principals, Mr. Juffs asked me to be the teacher sponsor of the Inter-School Christian Fellowship group. Unlike in Newmarket, this group quickly became the largest group that I had ever worked with. The classroom was full of eager, smiling young believers.

It was at the end of the first year when Cathy, our young son and I headed to the area in Michigan north of Midland. We were attending our first ever Fellowship of Christian Athletes conference. I received some solid basic coaching skills in baseball. These became my foundation for the next thirty years of coaching baseball. Of more importance than the skills learned, was the fact that each of the people in charge of a clinic began their sessions through prayer. In the fall of that year, I began the practice of having prayer before each game. I don't know how many other, if any, coaches in the public school system had followed a similar practice. I never prayed for us to win, but emphasized that we would give our best and enjoy ourselves. The significant factor was that we were involving God in our game.

In the years following this visit to this FCA camp, we would make a number of visits to FCA camps in Indiana, Michigan and Pennsylvania. The major highlight was that for two consecutive summers, we took our family, plus a van load of girls, to the national basketball camps at the national FCA conference grounds in Marshall, Indiana. These visits happened in the mid-nineteen seventies.

At this time, there were no Christian athlete camps in Canada. The Athletes in Action group began a few years later, developing from Canadian pro football.

One of the responsibilities I had at the school was to coordinate school assemblies. During the years Mr. Juffs was principal, I was able to invite speakers who stressed their Christian faith. This included a couple of visits from a group of four Toronto Argos who came as representatives of Athletes in Action.

———— LETTERS FROM RON ————

Who is our Source? In other words, who is our provider? It is certainly not any level, or any department of government. And yet in this day and age, many people are looking to the government to be their source.

When the original Beeton arena was built in the late 1940s and the Flesherton arena was built in the 1970s, both were built without promise of local government support. When the arena was built in Flesherton, there was even a council statement declaring no local tax money be used to build the arena.

In Flesherton, Ron Gostick and I became the two people in charge of raising this money. The shell of the arena went up, but the inside was completely unfinished. Over a period of almost twenty years, we were able to raise the money, complete the inside, as well as putting an extension on the building. No government at any level was the source. Neither Ron nor I were the source. We just provided leadership in the fundraising.

However, things have changed dramatically today. People look to government grants to provide for new local municipal buildings and fields. As a result, it seems that more and more people are looking to levels of government as the source.

We seem to think that the government can take care of environmental problems. Again, we look to the government to supply our safety. We have virtually taken God out of our public school system. We are destroying monuments of people who are not perfect, but who have been important for the continued development of our country through the years.

Because we are not looking at the true Source, our Heavenly Father, the world around us is collapsing at a very rapid pace.

Each and every one of us needs to let our God take back control, as our Source.

He loves each of us with a love that is beyond our understanding. He is as interested in each of us, as the most caring mother is with each of her children. It doesn't matter if we are talking about food on our table, a car accident, a person who was born severely handicapped, a hockey game, a stranger on the street. The list goes on and on. Our Heavenly Father is concerned for each of us.

He is the only Source who has all the answers. Each of our relationships is individual. Each of us needs to seek the Source for our situation. Others may talk to God to support us but in the end, it comes down to Him and the individual that He loves so very much.

——— Letters from Ron ———

We had lots of fun with our second child Rob as he grew into his own person. When he was a six-year-old, I would rush home from school and get him ready for his four p.m. hockey practice. We also had a family rule that when you began something, you were to finish it.

After rushing to get home and get Rob dressed, we would get to the arena and watch him out on the ice. He would be paying no attention to the coach. I watched this for three or four weeks. I became very frustrated. I called him over and told him to get off the ice. We were going home. In the car, I stated to Rob that he wasn't quitting hockey, I was. I would not be taking him back. The next week, Rob got his mother to take him to hockey. He went on the ice and became involved. We never had the problem again.

It was a couple of years later. The previous season, hockey took place one night, while the Cubs meeting was on a different night. Rob enjoyed both. However, this new year was different. Hockey and Cubs were both on the same night. Rob and I talked about it. I told him that he had to choose which activity to continue and which to leave behind. As our family was highly involved in hockey, I was certainly hoping that he would choose hockey. However, I was asking him to make his own decision. We discussed the situation three or four times. Rob chose hockey.

A couple of weeks later, Rob asked me if I was upset with him for choosing hockey. I assured him that I was not. At the same time, I was thanking my Heavenly Father that I had done my job.

Rob soon took up the sport of baseball. He immediately had a passion for this sport. He also did not like to fail at it. His temper showed when he struck out. He would take his helmet and throw it over the screen. This went on for almost half of the baseball season. I finally felt that enough was enough. I spoke to Rob and said, "You have a choice. You can play baseball, but if you throw your helmet over the screen once more, you will not be playing baseball". Rob's reply was that he didn't have a choice. He wanted to play baseball. As a result, he would no longer throw his helmet over the screen.

For the past fifteen plus years, Rob has been the head baseball coach first at Colorado Christian University and for the past seven years at Vanguard University in Costa Mesa, California.

CHAPTER 27

"IN THE COMMUNITY"

Two things that I have believed in since I was a child, are that Christianity is less about religion, or attending church and more about a seven day a week, twenty-four hour a day relationship with Jesus.

This leads to my second belief. As Christ gave His life to provide salvation for the entire population of the earth, a Christian needs to be a servant of Jesus in whatever task Jesus has given to that Christian to do. As has been stated many times already, young people are my lifeblood.

Minor Hockey in Flesherton had been operated by the Kinsmen. It was now decided that there should be a minor hockey organization. I became the Vice-President on the first executive of three people. When the President resigned halfway through the first season, I became the President. The husband of our Secretary-Treasurer, Joan Croft, literally strolled through the arena to recruit an additional five executive members.

I believed that it was important for me to be in charge of the developing organization. It would possess all of the features I believed were important for our growing son to play in. I would be an active executive member for the next twenty-five years. The organization was for the benefit of the kids.

Minor hockey needed an arena to play in. We had the shell of an arena. The shell was built, but only partially paid for. It was also necessary for the shell to be completed. As a result, I became part of the arena board. Ron Gostick and I led the board to raise money and complete the building. As a result, I was on the Arena Board for over a quarter of a century.

How do you raise these funds? Flesherton did not have any big business, or any stated millionaires. My history head was a village councillor and member of the arena board. He thought of the idea of a yearly festival. This became the Split Rail Festival.

The name and the idea all came from Mr. Little. I became the legs of the idea development. As a committee of one, I approached the council seeking approval to pursue the idea. When I got this, I chaired a public meeting to gain support. Then I wrote the original constitution of Split Rail.

I was not a member of the board of Split Rail, but my wife Cathy would be an original board member, staying on for over twenty-five years. I worked in the grass roots. At the first Split Rail Festival, Minor Hockey sold potatoes and apples. The potatoes had been planted by minor hockey kids in a farmer's field. The potatoes had been donated by Elmgrove area farmers, just outside of Alliston. I was working with some of their baseball teams. Under the leadership of Garney Reed, the potatoes were harvested by minor hockey kids. The Collingwood area apples were picked by minor hockey kids after school hours.

In the second year of the festival, Minor Hockey took charge of the turkey supper, which ran for the entire history of Split Rail. The supper often fed over six hundred people. As a result, the Split Rail became a major fundraiser for the kids in minor hockey. This helped to keep the registration fees lower.

The Split Rail Foundation made major donations toward developing the interior of the arena. This donation was important in keeping ice rental rates to Minor Hockey low.

The main benefactors were the kids and their families.

Minor hockey developed a family rate for registration. As my memory recalls, the first two children from a family paid the regular rate, the third and fourth member paid less, and any other members were free. It is important to emphasize that the arena operated in the black during these years.

Other than the minor hockey fundraising effort at Split Rail, the girls' basketball teams ran an ice cream booth. The now world-famous Chapman's Ice Cream was just starting out as a small family business in Markdale. In cooperation with the infant ice cream company, the girls worked to raise money for their tournaments and travel. Again, the people who benefited most were the young girls just starting to emerge as a basketball dynasty.

CHAPTER 28

"HE IS LORD"

The many Bible based churches in the area of the school provided the majority of the students who formed the strong InterSchool Christian Fellowship group. Within these churches and even beyond, were many families with strong Christian Biblical roots.

I was asked by Mrs. Robinson in our first year in the village to become the Sunday School superintendent at St. Johns United Church. I declined.

During my last years in Beeton, the United Church had come out with the New Curriculum for Sunday Schools. Like many others, I was completely opposed to the Curriculum. I even spoke out about it from the pulpit, whenever I was the speaker for a service.

United Church Sunday Schools across Canada lost many of their Sunday School teachers. They left the Church. Others of us were founding members of the United Church Renewal Fellowship, which had the purpose of working to renew the church from within.

The Sunday School in Flesherton had been affected like the rest of the Sunday Schools across Canada. It was in need of a major rebuilding, which would include replacing the New Curriculum with a different one.

It was a couple of years later, when I had become a board member at the church. We were in search of a new minister. When Reverend Wally

Leeman was interviewed, he said that he was aware of the charismatic movement which was growing in many churches in Canada. He said that he was interested in it. Following his interview, I moved that we hire Rev. Leeman as our minister. The Board voted to invite him to come.

Later in the year, at a meeting held in the home of Tom and Joan Magee. I agreed to become Sunday School superintendent. One of the ideas that was circulated was to try and get people to share the teaching of classes. I could not agree with this idea. If we wanted children to be dedicated to attending Sunday School, we needed to have full-time teachers, with an available supply teacher on standby.

All of our teachers became full-time teachers. We found an acceptable curriculum. We had a new minister, whose wife became very active in the Sunday School. The Sunday School began to grow. When I retired as the Superintendent, I was replaced by Peter and Georgia Symons, Jane Morrison and Diane Carlson.

Many of the young people in the Sunday School were the same people who were at hockey, baseball (another story!) basketball, also attending public, or high school together.

The church pews on Sunday mornings were occupied by a number of teachers from the high school and Macphail Public School.

During the decades of the late 1970s and the 1980s, I was a member of the board, serving as chair for six years.

In 1979, a revival campaign was held in the auditorium at the high school. It was sponsored by many of the churches in the Flesherton area. There were a number of prayer groups, who prayed primarily for revival. Pastor Michael Liew from Cedarside Baptist and I co-chaired the event.

One of the outcomes of the crusade was the South East Grey Praise Fellowship beginning to meet monthly each Sunday evening. The meetings were held at St. Johns. For a number of years, the church was full for the guest speaker and musicians coming to lead worship. A number of people, including some teenagers, accepted Christ as Lord and Saviour.

CHAPTER 29

"THE HOLY SPIRIT"

I grew up very aware of the Trinity that is our God. Our church in Beeton is Beeton Trinity United Church. As I was growing up, the church service always began with the singing of Holy, Holy, Holy. One of the lines of this hymn refers to God in Three Persons, Blessed Trinity. I was also aware that Jesus had gone to be with His Father in Heaven. He was replaced in this world by the Holy Spirit. This meant that when a person accepts Jesus as their Lord and Saviour, it is actually Jesus in the form of the Holy Spirit who comes to live within us. I was very aware that the Holy Spirit was living in me.

I was not aware that there was a power that could be added to a person's life by a personal event called the baptism of the Holy Spirit.

There is no question that God was taking His time in my life in having this happen.

When I went by myself to hear Pastor Hall in the Orange Hall in Beeton, these meetings were my introduction. I was a ten-year-old at the time. It was thirty years later that I came to realize that this was my introduction. I still have the song book that I purchased. The songs are the songs of the Holy Spirit.

During my first year at Huron Heights, I was invited by the ISCF group at Banting to come back and speak. The invitation came from Wayne Wardell, who was now President of the group. After the meeting,

Wayne and I had a lengthy talk. He asked me if I had experienced the baptism of the Holy Spirit. I assured him that the Holy Spirit lived in me, as I had accepted Christ as Lord and Saviour. However, Wayne was not satisfied with my answer. He kept coming back about the baptism. When our discussion ended, I was still assuring Wayne of the presence of the Holy Spirit in my life. Wayne was still asking me if I had received the baptism of the Holy Spirit.

In our third year at Grey Highlands a bus load of ISCF members went to the Catacombs of Toronto in an Anglican Church on Bloor Street. The Catacombs was all about the charismatic movement. The evening was a life changing event for a number of our group. Jesus became a major part of their life.

We also met Dave and Marg Hinds, who then came to Flesherton for a couple of weekends of meetings. These were meetings held at St. Johns and sponsored by the ISCF group. The Hinds did speak at the Sunday morning church service. On both of their visits, the Hinds stayed with us.

On the first visit, Dave and I got into a discussion in which he asked me if I had accepted Jesus as my Saviour. My immediate response was "yes". He then asked me if I had experienced the baptism of the Holy Spirit. I hesitated. I wasn't sure. The conversation carried on. David showed me many Scriptures. I received the baptism of the Holy Spirit that afternoon.

At the service that evening, my wife received the baptism. She immediately received the gift of speaking in tongues, which is one of the signs that you have received the baptism. It was a couple of weeks later while talking to God in the bathroom, that I received the gift of tongues.

As soon as I received the Holy Spirit's baptism, I found myself with much more power in my daily living. I was a much better servant for Jesus.

The acceptance of the baptism of the Holy Spirit has no connection to a person's salvation. It is the way a person can serve Jesus and the Holy Trinity at a more dedicated level.

I speak almost daily in tongues, as part of my private time with my God.

According to my understanding, the Holy Spirit is speaking through me, for me and at a level that I am not capable of reaching. This talk with my Heavenly Father allows me to live a closer life to Him.

CHAPTER 30

"A SURPRISE"

God loves to surprise His children. He loves to give His child gifts. One of the gifts that God gave me was baseball.

I had been involved in playing and coaching baseball for almost two decades, when we moved to Flesherton. I was part of the administration of the sport both locally and at the provincial level. I thought that I would probably not be a coach in Flesherton. At the time, there wasn't even a diamond. However, under the leadership of Bob Elliott the Kinsmen began constructing a diamond behind the arena. Jamie was now six years old. I asked him if he wanted to play soccer, or baseball. I said that I would work to develop his sport in Flesherton. If he chose soccer, there were a number of coaches available. However if he chose baseball, there were not many coaches.

Jamie chose baseball. The rest is history. We lost our first ball game in Midland 43 – 1. There were no mercy rules. However, by nineteen eighty-five, Flesherton was beginning to win provincial championships. In the next fifteen years, Flesherton had more Ontario championship teams and finalists than any other village, or small town in Ontario.

Although there was a dry spell for local baseball in the early years of the century, through the diligent efforts of Barb Henry, there has been a major revival. In 2019 Mary Green won the provincial award as the most outstanding player in the thirteen and under category. Her father

Kevin played in that first game in Midland. Her grandmother Doreen Green, who was very active for many years at St. Johns, was a member of our first baseball executive.

In nineteen seventy-six, I became the volunteer executive director of Ontario Baseball. The office was in our home. I had earlier earned my Master's Degree in educational planning, so I could work to become a principal. This was not God's plan. I would use my degree to administrate baseball in Ontario.

During my second year as the administrator, the President Jack Lee introduced a prayer to open each executive meeting. During the next twenty years, I would be asked to lead in this prayer every meeting. This includes the Annual Meetings, where I also said grace at the banquet.

We began a church service on the Sunday morning of the annual convention in 1976. This is still carried on today. There have seldom been more than ten people at the service, but it is a living witness.

It happened that some of the executive members who had various family problems, came to me to discuss these problems.

It seemed that I had become the organization's padre, as well as the chief administrator.

Ontario Baseball has often had over ten thousand young people playing the sport in the summer season.

As we wrote at the beginning of this chapter, God never showed me that this baseball happening was going to take place.

It is certainly one of the greatest gifts in my life.

CHAPTER 31

"THIS AND THAT"

A ll sunshine makes a desert. In other words, problems in life help us to grow, as rain is important for most plant growth.

God had always led me to be part of the United Church. When the issue of sex between people of the same gender became an issue, it led to our church at St. Johns being split. I was chair of the board and chaired the meeting when I knew there would soon be another meeting to decide on opening a new church. I knew on which side God had led my wife and I to stand. I did not want this to influence anyone else. Each person's decision would be between that person and God. As a result, I was very careful how I worded my leadership at the meeting.

When we announced at Sunday church service we would be staying at St. Johns, many of the evangelicals who were leaving were very upset at us. The criticism we received was probably the most severe ever directed at us. We were only doing what God asked us to do.

In the years following, Rev. Martin Garniss came to our church. I once again became Sunday School Superintendent. We were able to rebuild the Sunday School and the church. We were greatly helped by three different visits of the Masters Commission from Phoenix, Arizona. St. Johns often worked in cooperation with the Country Gospel Church from Dundalk. David and Margo Watson were their pastors.

Many, many young people had life changing experiences. A number have gone on to provide leadership in a variety of churches and other Christ related activities.

I had been led by the Lord to proclaim the gospel in the United Church of Canada for over fifty years. I often disagreed with the policies of the central church.

It is approaching ten years ago, that a new policy of the church became one that boycotted some of the activity of Israel. These people are God's chosen people.

The Bible is very definite in stating that those people who bless the Jewish race will be blessed, but those who harm these chosen people will suffer the consequences.

There was no question for me. It was necessary to leave the United Church. The decision had absolutely nothing to do with any of the people. It was strictly related to the church policy.

We have maintained our relationship with friends who are in the United Church. On a number of occasions, I have accepted invitations to speak in United Churches as I did for the previous fifty years. To God be the Glory.

─────── LETTERS FROM RON ───────

As we watched the two-day funeral of the late George Bush Senior, we couldn't help feeling how much this world has changed since Mr. Bush was President thirty years ago.

There is no question that Mr. Bush lived a life dedicated to serving his God, his wife, his family and his country, in this order. He realized that it was of utmost importance to put the love of God first, so that he would have the love from God to love his wife, family and country.

This is the major change in the society of 1990 and the society of today. Churches used to be full on Sunday in 1990, but today these same churches are closing their doors almost daily. Many of the people who really are Christians will claim a love for God, but worshipping Him and talking with Him get set aside for other things, including travelling, shopping, cutting the lawn, a round of golf and the list just goes on and on. God must be given His proper place in order, so that our lives can be properly lived. The chaos of today is because this place of His doesn't have lots of Christians. There are many others who need to accept God into their life.

Personally, a simple example is my coaching. As many of you know, this person loved coaching. He either loved it, or he was completely crazy, having coached two hundred and thirteen teams over a period of forty-nine years. By the grace of God, many of these teams were very successful. Seven of the boys that I was an early coach of went on to play in the N.H.L. Some have been finalists, or winners of the Stanley Cup.

In the year two thousand and nineteen, I really doubt that if I were a young person today, I would want to coach. It's a different world.

Those in authority in sports insist that a future coach needs to attend clinic after clinic, taught by people who have never won anything. Many of these clinicians do not even understand what winning is about. These same sport leaders insist on having many events on Sunday, making it difficult for a young family to worship. Flesherton ran at least seven tournaments in hockey each year for almost thirty years. No game was ever scheduled for Sunday. The tournaments were always full and always successful.

And then there are the parents. Because they have watched hockey on TV, many consider themselves experts. A concept I used to espouse was "parents bring your children to the arena for practice and then go home." The sport is for the fun of the child and the satisfaction of the parent.

Yes, Mr. Bush. It is a very different world today.

CHAPTER 32

"2020"

Following our separation from the United Church, we began worshipping at St. Andrews Presbyterian Church in Priceville. During the years that have followed, we have had a very enjoyable time of fellowship. My major contribution has been as guest speaker in the pulpit two, or three times each summer.

In August of this year, we moved from our home in Flesherton to a brand-new condo in Mount Forest. We had not been in Mount Forest for more than a total of seven weeks, as the year 2019 came to a close. We have been travelling and visiting our children and grandchildren.

However, we have already become involved in the First Baptist Church in Mount Forest, where the congregation has been described as having come from many other churches and denominations. I have already met people there who were part of the United Church in Mount Forest, when I spoke back in the late 1980s. We have had fellowship with friends from the Letterbeen United Church, where I have spoken many times going back to when I was a student at University and my roommate Alex Taylor was its minister.

We have not moved to Mount Forest to retire, but are in this beautiful town for new beginnings. Of course, there is no question that we are completely in God's hands. His plan is one day at a time.

I am very happy for the internet, Facebook and today's telephone services. Through these various electrical devices, I can almost daily be in touch with our children and grandchildren in Saskatchewan, California and Texas. I am able to instantly wish "Happy Birthday" to many former students, as well as many friends. I am also able to follow many of the happenings in their life. Even in small ways, I can be involved in events in Beeton and Flesherton, regardless of where we are in the world.

Much of this involvement is with former students, some of whom are in their sixties and seventies. It also includes involvement with grand nieces and nephews in their late twenties and thirties.

If God so desires, I will be entering my sixty sixth year of lay supply preaching. When we are at our daughters and son-in-law's home in Texas, I am a greeter for children's church. I look forward to this hour when I give high-fives to a number of the seven hundred children who attend. I sit on my walker and am thrilled when a three-year-old comes bursting into the church, running at full speed to me to give me a high-five. Yes, kids are still my lifeblood. The difference today is, the kids vary in age from two and three to over seventy.

And for Cathy and I, the very, very important group to us are our fourteen Grandbabies.

Thank you, Heavenly Father, Jesus and Holy Spirit.

CHAPTER 33

THE KEYS

Jesus had been Lord and Saviour of my life for over seventy-five years. During that time, although I am far from being Christlike, I have tried with His and the Holy Spirit's help and guidance to be a good servant.

The importance of prayer, which I discovered at my mother's knee, has increased in my life with every passing year. My prayers are not for me, but for my extended family, my friends including those of over seventy years. I pray for people that have not always agreed with me, nor I with them. Revival will come if we will humble ourselves in prayer to the Holy Trinity. As one great theologian has stated, the three are all family. It does not matter which one we pray to.

This praying is part of the time I spend daily with God. As my mobility has declined, I find myself spending more and more time with just the Holy Spirit.

There are no other keys. As an old chorus goes, God answers prayer in the morning, God answers prayer at noon, God answers prayer in the evening.

This prayer will keep your heart in tune.

—— Letters from Ron ——

What has been the biggest highlight of our forty-eight years in Flesherton? The answer is simple. For me, it has been watching our three children and their mother develop into very strong individuals in their own right. Jamie was born in Newmarket, but came here as a one year old. Rob and Stacey were both born in Markdale hospital. Like their Mother, the three have felt free to develop their own personality and life. Each of us, as individuals, and as a family have enjoyed life to its fullest in Flesherton.

When Jamie was fifteen, he began leaving the community each year to play hockey and to go to school. He returned to this community each summer. His journey took him to Waterloo and his sixth Ontario Championship.

He then went to Peterborough, where his team won a seventh Ontario Championship and the right to compete for the Memorial Cup. It was then off to Calgary and its university, where his team twice won the Western University championship and had the opportunity of playing for the Canadian University championship.

After school, he spent a year playing hockey in Norway, another year in England, a year in Texas, another year in West Virginia and a final season divided between Georgia and Tennessee. While at the University of Calgary, he met a girl from a strong Christian home in Saskatchewan. He married Tara and he is the General Manager of the family farm equipment company in Frontier, Saskatchewan. Jamie is often the guest speaker at the Lutheran Church that he attends, along with Tara and their eight children. Torin is the second oldest and has also spoken at the church on different occasions.

Rob completed high school here as an Ontario Scholar. He also assisted his father as Superintendent of the United Church Sunday School. With math as his major, he could have gone to almost any University in Canada, but he wanted to try baseball. After a visit to Arizona, he applied to, then was accepted at, Scottsdale Community College. This school is a junior college. He attended the school's baseball program as a walk on. He eventually made their team. After his third year at the junior college, he received a full scholarship from what has become known as Vanguard University. Rob's scholarship was partially academic and partially baseball. In his first year, he was named the NAIA western male athlete of the year. His wife-to-be, Angela, is an outstanding young Christian who attended Vanguard on a full basketball scholarship. Vanguard is known as a Christian school, under the guidance of the United States Pentecostal Church. Rob has now been Head Coach at Vanguard for seven years, after spending time as head coach at Colorado Christian. He did play one season of professional ball in Canton, Ohio. The team won the league championship. Rob has also achieved a master's degree with the subject of Theology being a significant part of it. Rob, Angela and their four children live in Anaheim and I am out of space. Next time, the female side.

——— Letters from Ron ———

On the last Sunday in August 2019, the Reverend David Nicholson and his bride, Marie celebrated their sixty year marriage during the Sunday morning service at St. Andrew's Presbyterian in Priceville. Marie performed her usual job playing the organ and piano. David conducted the service, spoke briefly and played his violin as a major part of the worship.

When David was speaking, he made reference to an article that he had read on top of a desk in a doctor's office in Pembroke. He had asked for a copy and they obliged by running one off for him. The article has no known author and no known source. In fact, Rev, Nicholson's copy may be one of the only copies in existence; I asked Rev. Nicholson if I could share this article with my readers. He was happy to have this happen...

Count Your Blessings

If you have food in the refrigerator, clothes on your back, a roof over your head and a place to sleep . . . You are richer than 75% of this world.

If you have money in the bank, in your wallet, and spare change in a dish somewhere . . . You are among the top 8% of the world's wealthy.

If you woke up this morning with more health, than illness . . .

You are more blessed than the million who will not even survive this week.

If you have never experienced the danger of battle, the loneliness of imprisonment, the agony of torture, or the pangs of starvation...

You are ahead of 500 million people in the world.

If you can attend a church meeting without fear of harassment, arrest, torture, or death...You are more blessed than three billion people in the world.

If your parents are still alive and still married...You are very rare, even in North America.

If you hold up your head with a smile on your face and are truly thankful...You are blessed because although the majority can, most do not.

If you can hold someone's hand, hug them or even touch them on the shoulder...You are blessed because you can offer healing touch.

If you can read this message, you just received a double blessing in that someone was thinking of you, and furthermore, you are more blessed than over two billion people in the world that cannot read at all.

Have a good day, count your blessings and pass along this to remind everyone else how blessed you are.

Thanks David. May you and Marie have many more years sharing your love.

———— Letters from Ron ————

Joel Olsteen is the pastor of a large church in Houston, Texas. He also has a large TV ministry and is often asked to be a guest at conferences. Recently, a comment about Joel was made on TV that was not complimentary. In fact, in this day and age such comments often lead to the person who has made the comment being taken to court.

When Joel, who is very much a fan of positive thinking, was asked if he would be taking this person to court, Joel responded that he is too blessed to even think about it.

Oswald J. Smith was the founder and pastor of the People's Church in Toronto. In the 1950's this very missions orientated church gave more annually to foreign missions, than many of the traditional denominations did from all of their churches across Canada. One of Dr. Oswald J's comments was that we will let our critics go about criticizing us and we will go about doing the job that God has given to us to do.

Following one of the thousands of crusade meetings, through which hundreds of thousands of people have come to a personal relationship with Jesus, a person spoke to Billy Graham and stated that he didn't like Mr. Graham's methods. Billy asked him what methods he had. The man replied that he didn't have a method. Billy responded that he liked his methods much better.

Dwight Moody was a shoe salesman in Chicago in the mid-1800s, who became an evangelist. Mr. Moody had large crowds wherever he went. Following one of his meetings, a man approached him and said that he had made one hundred and twenty-eight grammar errors in his sermon that night. Mr. Moody responded that he is using all the English he knows to the glory of God. Could this person say the same?

Mr. Moody made it a habit to witness personally to at least one person a day. There was the day that he was going to bed in his Chicago home, when he realized that he had not witnessed to anyone that day. He put on his housecoat and went out to a lamppost in front of his home. When he witnessed to a man about Jesus, the man asked him what business it was of his. Mr. Moody responded that he was Dwight Moody. The man replied that indeed it was his business.

Dwight Moody had an amazing reputation.

CHAPTER 33

MORE LETTERS OF FAITH

—— Letters from Ron ——

Jesus did not come to give us a religion. He had no such intention. He also didn't come to give us a physical building called a church. Again, He had no such plan.

Why did Jesus come? He had one great purpose and that was to give us a personal relationship with our three Triune God: God the Father, God the Holy Spirit and Himself, God the Son.

In the day and age that we are living in, there are many people in our area, as well as much of the rest of Canada, who used to attend a church building on a fairly regular basis, but no longer attend. This is very interesting because many of these people have a faith and a relationship with Jesus. In many cases, these people no longer find the church building that they used to attend to be relevant. Many also have no use for the politics that are part of this church building. In other words, many of these people are part of the church of Jesus Christ, but have no communications with a religious denomination.

It was almost a century ago, the ballplayer Billy Sunday, who became a great evangelist in his day, stated that hell will be so full of hypocrites attending the physical church each Sunday, that their feet will be sticking out the windows. In other words, many people who attend the physical church structure do not have a relationship with Jesus.

Let's go back to those people who do have a relationship with Jesus, but who do not attend the physical church structure. The worst result of this is that in our society, many children have not received any teaching about their parents' relationship with Jesus. The children have not come to know who Jesus is. This appears to be part of the reason that the society we live in today is becoming more and more godless, where many ideas and socially accepted practices not being what Jesus, who loves us so much, would have us follow.

Jesus did intend for His followers to get together to study His Word. He did intend that His followers would have a fellowship of love. In the early days following the time of Jesus' life on earth, this fellowship became called the church. The longer society has gone on, the more the church building has become confused with what the fellowship of believers was and is meant to be.

There is no greater need in the society of today than to have the fellowship of Jesus become a growing part of this society.

We will then see in our day to day living, the love of Jesus.

———— LETTERS FROM RON ————

Many of you are familiar with the story of Isaac and Abraham. Isaac is the child promised by God to be the beginning of a large Nation. God called on Abraham to sacrifice Isaac on an altar. This seemed to be a contradiction of God's promise. However, the very faithful Abraham obeyed. He bound Isaac and was ready to place him on the altar, when a lamb appeared in the brush and an angel told Abraham that the lamb was to take Isaac's place. Abraham was being tested. He passed the test with flying colours.

It was some centuries later. The Nation of which Isaac was the first born, had virtually become slaves in the land of the Egyptians. Moses had been trying to negotiate their freedom. The leader of the Egyptians continued to promise and then go back on his word.

This led to the origin of the feast of the Passover. God told the Israelites that in each house that they lived, they were to take a perfect lamb with absolutely no blemishes, kill the lamb and with the blood of this perfect lamb, put a mark over the door of their home. That night the angel of death was coming to the land of Egypt. A child would die in each home, unless the angel saw the blood mark. In this case, the angel would pass over the home. The blood of the perfect lamb saved a child from death.

These two events are a couple of great examples of how the Bible is completely coordinated. It is the Word of God.

Each of these stories are examples of how God used the lamb, many, many centuries before Jesus was born, to illustrate the life of Jesus.

Jesus is the perfect lamb, who took away the sins of each of us. God did not allow Abraham's son to die. He sent a substitute. He did allow His only Son to come and die.

Like the lambs in the Passover, Jesus was a perfect lamb. He had no blemishes. His blood was shed.

As the Scripture states "As in Adam all died, so in Christ everyone is redeemed." The blood has washed away each of our blemishes, if we accept this unbelievable sacrifice.

Christ died, but on the third day He rose from the dead. Many people saw the resurrected Christ. Thomas, one of the disciples, had not seen the risen Jesus. Thomas stated that he needed to see the nail prints in the hands of Jesus, in order for him to believe. When Jesus appeared in the presence of Thomas, Jesus stated that it is good that you believe, because you have seen.

However, it is even greater that many who have not seen, have and are believing.

Jesus is risen. He is risen indeed.

———— LETTERS FROM RON ————

The "Great I AM" is the Holy God. He is also known as Jehovah. During the years that I was growing up and even in my late twenties and mid thirties, we always began our morning church service singing "Holy, Holy, Holy Lord God almighty. Early in the morning, our song does rise to Thee. Holy, Holy Holy, merciful and mighty. God in Three Persons, Blessed Trinity".

It is very interesting and significant that the Father God of Christianity is always referred to in the Bible as the Holy God. He is not called the great God of love. He is called the Holy One.

This does not mean that He is not loving, because He does love each and every one of His human creations with a love that really is beyond the understanding of the human mind. In the gospel song "Amazing Grace", the word love could easily be used instead of grace. Regardless of what any one of us may have done, The Great I AM" will continue to love each and every human being. He doesn't appreciate many of the things that humans have done, but He never stops, or even hesitates, loving the person.

The question must be raised since He is so loving why is He referred to as the Holy God? The answer is very simple. It is because His love is wrapped up in His Holiness. His love cannot be taken out of the boundary of His Holiness.

It was and is the reason that it was necessary for His Son Jesus, to come into this world and live perfect without sin (or disobedience to the Holy One), in order that the price of each human's disobedience could be paid. The Holiness of God demanded that this perfect life of His Son would require the shedding of His Son's blood, in order that each and every human could reunite with our Holy God.

In the year 2018, the Holiness of God is difficult to find in our North American society. The church no longer sings "Holy, Holy, Holy" as part of the regular Sunday morning service. The church may choose to not even sing of God's Holiness. What was once the Sabbath, is now the weekend. Many are the people who not only do not attend a Sunday service, but many are the people who do not even think of God during the entire weekend.

Our society has almost completely set aside the Holy God, but He is still there patiently waiting, for who knows how long. The day is coming when the Holy One will allow the very things that our society has put in His place, to destroy this society.

——— Letters from Ron ———

Jesus is the Light of the World. In the third chapter of the gospel of John, the Bible states that the world was in darkness until Jesus came. However, there are those who prefer the darkness. The individuals who prefer darkness, reject the life, death and resurrection of Jesus.

The many lights of Christmas are a great proclamation that Jesus is the light.

Through the years we have gone out into the various places that we have been, to see the Christmas lights that people have put up on their homes. We have seen beautiful lights in Anaheim, Denver, Scottsdale and Dallas. We have gone a number of times on a wagon ride in Dallas. The farm wagon is pulled by a team of horses. The ride goes through a number of streets, where most of the homes have wonderful decorations highlighted by the lights.

The lights and decorations must cost thousands of dollars. The owners of the homes are apparently prepared to pay the price to have their home decorated. When the baby Jesus came, He came for the purpose of dying. It was necessary for Him to live a sinless life. He had to leave His home in Heaven. He was born in complete humility in a stable. One group of His visitors at His birth were shepherds. This was at a time that shepherds were considered to be one of the lowest forms of human life. Many people would not associate with a shepherd. It was not a glamourous job.

The second group were scientists, who had come from many miles away. They were following a star. They were also following a story about an amazing birth, that would conclude their journey.

A third group proclaimed the birth of Jesus, as they lit up the sky for the shepherds. This group came from Heaven. These were the angels who proclaimed Jesus' birth to the lowly shepherds. Glory to God in the highest.

The birth of Jesus was and is unbelievable to some people. The mother of the baby was a young woman who was still a virgin. The Father of Jesus was another member of the Blessed Trinity. His Father is the Holy Ghost. The responsibility of Fatherhood is just one of the multitude of functions that the amazing Holy Spirit has performed and continues daily to perform.

The Light of the World provides for anyone who wants it. His light provides peace that goes beyond understanding. He also is the road to eternal life.

The next major function that the Holy Spirit has played after His Fatherhood role is to be with each person who has accepted the Light of the World. With the little light that a believer becomes, the person can brighten the corner where the person is.

——— LETTERS FROM RON ———

It was in 1972 when my Mother's back began to bother her. With each passing day, the back pain got worse and worse. Mom did not like going to the doctor. Eventually, the pain became so bad that she had little choice. Tests showed that Mother was suffering from breast cancer. An operation took place. Remember, this was the year 1972. Some of the cancer cells were removed, but Mom was not in very good shape. After a few weeks in the Toronto hospital, she returned to the Alliston hospital. The head nurse in Alliston was a good friend of my wife's family. She told my wife's brother that she had not seen a worse case of cancer for a long time. My Mom was given only a couple of months to live.

It was a couple of weeks after this that I went to visit Mom. As I was entering the door to her room, Mother could be heard crying out that she wished she was dead, she wished that she was dead.

I sat down at Mom's bedside and it suddenly hit me like a ton of bricks that here we sat, the two of us. We both believed in the power of prayer, but we had never prayed about Mother's sickness. Almost unbelievable. I took her hand. I began praying for her. I prayed to God that Mom had always been His little girl. She always loved Him and always tried to honour Him. I just asked Him in Jesus' name, to love and cuddle His little girl. I stressed this to God in two or three different ways.

When I finished, my mother who was the greatest cheerleader of her son, quoted from the Book of James, she said, "The effectual fervent prayer of a righteous man does a lot of good." I began coming to the hospital each Sunday morning and listening with my mother to one of her favourite TV gospel programs. I never heard her cry out again. She began putting on weight. As spring approached, she returned to her own home.

At this same time, she had developed cataracts on both her eyes. She could not see. I made arrangements to take her to a cataract specialist. He said that he could not operate on a terminal case. Mother was classified as a terminal case.

It was a couple of weeks later that I took Mom to an appointment with her cancer specialist. At the conclusion of the appointment the specialist stated, "She might as well be operated on because nothing is happening here." In the early fall, my mother saw two of her grandchildren for the first time, even though both were a little over a year old. She had continued to put on weight.

It was a year after this that I took Mother for an appointment at the Alliston hospital. One of the administrators in the office spoke to me and said, "that woman is a miracle." It was only a short time after this that my Dad died.

Mom's life was wrapped up in her husband of over fifty years. She lost her will to live. Less than three months later, my Mom died of a massive heart attack.

———— Letters from Ron ————

It was in the late 1970s. Benny Hinn, who was an evangelist and faith healer came to speak in this area on a number of occasions. We heard him at Full Gospel in Orangeville. We had heard him in Owen Sound. We had gone as far south as Guelph on another occasion.

We were once again in Owen Sound on a Sunday night. At the conclusion of his spoken message, Benny gave a call for anyone with back problems to stand up for the purpose of receiving healing. He then asked those who had stood up to come forward to the altar.

My wife had been suffering from severe back pain for over a year. She had been to a number of doctors, chiropractors and other people who treated back problems. She still had severe back pain. When Benny asked those with back pain to stand, she stood up. She went to the altar. When she got there, Benny's team prayed for her. She slumped to the ground. She had been what is called slain in the spirit. She was not pushed or forced. After a few minutes, she stirred and sat up. She then got to her feet and talked to a member of the team. She returned to her seat. She said that she thought the pain had disappeared.

The days passed by. The weeks passed by. The months passed by. Then the years passed by. She gave birth to a little girl who this year celebrated her fortieth birthday.

In the year 2019, my wife likes to play golf two or three times a week. Since the day at the healing crusade, she has never seen a medical person about her back. She has suffered no pain. She enjoys going for long walks.

There is absolutely no question that the healing power of God is at work in this world today. There is no question that God the Father, God the Son and God the Holy Spirit, the great 3-in-1 is still in charge. He loves each of us as His little child. He loves you and He loves me. He is amazing.

——— Letters from Ron ———

A multitude of thanks to our Heavenly Father. It is the thanksgiving season. In the New Testament, it states "seek ye first the Kingdom of God and His Righteousness and all these things will be added unto you."

It seems that in this day and age the great majority, even the majority of Christians, want and want all the things the world seems to offer, without first seeking God and His righteousness. As a result, their things do not come, or if they do come, not in the way the seeker anticipated.

Our heavenly Father does not say anything in jest. He is very sincere when He states that we are to seek the Kingdom of God and His righteousness. This definitely must be our priority. When this happens, then our God fills our waiting "stockings" with more abundance of gifts that any of us really deserve.

In the Book of Malachi, the word of God talks about giving to God. The Word states that we are to bring all the tithe to God. We are not to hold back anything. It is at this time that we need to remember that you and I cannot outgive God. Our loving Heavenly Father just keeps giving and giving.

The scripture in Malachi continues by stating, if we give at least the tithe to God, He will open the floodgates, so that each of us will receive so many gifts, we will not have enough room for all of them.

The scripture reads "Test Me." That is a very strong statement.

In the book of Luke in the New Testament we read "Give and it will be given unto you". That which is given to you will be pressed down, shaken together and running over. God will give to you as you give to others, plus more.

Thanksgiving is not really about what we receive. It is about what we give.

Each of us has a different place and different cause to give to.

In order to have great joy in life, we definitely need to give and give and give again.

There is no lack of causes to give to. In truth, none of us can afford not to give.

Selfishness kills. Giving gives life and more life – and remember you can't out give God.

—— Letters from Ron ——

We were expecting our third child. We had two healthy boys aged nine and six years. The doctor brought our brand new, still not cleaned up, baby girl to me in the waiting room. I was overjoyed that we had our baby girl. I went in to see her mother. In the sixty-one years that I have known Cathy, she has never beamed more brightly than she did as she said to me "It's a girl."

It was a year and a half later. Stacey became very sick with the flu. Her body was almost limp when she was lifted up. This was very interesting. When each of her brothers were born, it was not long after their birth that I dedicated each of them to the Lord. In many ways, it was similar to Samuel's dedication by his mother. I had not done this with Stacey. She was my little girl. However, on this day when she was so sick, I went outside of our home and began walking around it. As I walked, God and I started talking. Stacey was given that day to the Lord. Within hours, the flu bug left her body completely.

We now fast forward to when our daughter was in her late twenties. She suffered a major heart attack, which was caused by the interior lining in one of her major arteries collapsing. It is a very unusual cause for a heart attack. We have since found out that the death rate from such an attack is eighty five percent.

This happened right near Dallas' major heart hospital. One of America's top heart surgeons was there to operate on Stacey. There were also over forty friends from the Masters Commission, which Stacey was a leader in, plus a number of the Alcala family. Cathy and I were visiting on this February 8th Sunday.

Every one of the people who were there prayed for Stacey to come through this event except her father (me). I could not take our daughter back from my Heavenly Father to whom I had given her twenty-five plus years ago. I had complete peace as my prayer to her Father and mine, was that she was His and she was in His hands. It was an experience very similar to the one that Abraham had with Isaac, when God provided a sheep at the last minute for the sacrifice.

Stacey is every bit as good an athlete as her brothers. She won the Arizona State championship in the 100-yard hurdles. She was the star of the game, when her girls' basketball team won the Arizona State quarterfinals.

My wife Cathy? Many of you know her. I need say nothing more.

ALSO BY RON PEGG

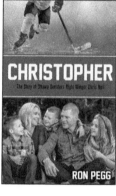

Christopher: The Story of Ottawa Senators Right Winger Chris Neil
9 978-1-4866-1672-5
Word Alive Press, 2018

Chris Neil—or Christopher, as his mother, Bonnie, called him—grew up with the ambition and desire to be an NHL hockey player. Through grit and determination, he achieved his goal and left an indelible mark on the Ottawa Senators franchise.

Christopher spent many hours as a youngster in Ron and Cathy Pegg's home, providing the author with personal, first-hand knowledge of Neil the hockey player and the man. That friendship continues to this day. In this engaging biography, you'll meet the Neil family and the personalities from the world of hockey that guided and formed Chris Neil throughout his life—a life of athletics, community involvement, and faith.

Bognor Bill: A Grey County Maverick
978-1-4866-1316-8
Word Alive Press, 2016

"I knew I wanted a front-row seat on [Bill's] re-election campaign in 2003. The man was a local legend, and my journalistic curiosity naturally drove me to question how much of it was myth. To the outsiders, the riding of Bruce-Grey-Owen Sound was at times insignificant, but the Bognor native who represented it was not."

"The only time I've seen MPP Murdoch pause reflectively was when he talked a bout the hardship, the work ethic, and the pride of his people at home. And that's what he liked to call them: my people. I never doubted he had his people's back. That was one part of his genius. He had Bruce and Grey born and bred in his bones and always had the pulse of his people's needs and wants. The other part of his genius was that he truly listened to the people, albeit he didn't always agree with them."

–Ana Sajfert
Legislative Aide, Queens Park

Here's Mrs. A: Canada's Woman of the 21st Century
978-1-4866-0500-2
Word Alive Press, 2014

Kate Aiken's young life experiences in Beeton were of the utmost importance in molding her into Canada's beloved "Mrs. A". Dubbed by her CFRB co-host Gordon Sinclair as the busiest woman in the world, she was a feminine dynamo who shared each of her experiences with her audience who loved her for what she was.

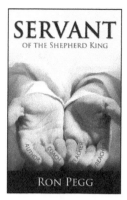

Servant of the Shepherd King
978-1-77069-557-3
Word Alive Press, 2012
Can one servant make a difference?
"Ron Pegg has been a beacon of light for his family, friends, school, neighbors, church, various sorts and community. His love for God is obvious, and is love for humankind is expressed in his mission to the community and beyond. He has been a support and mentor to many people, including myself. You will enjoy reading about the life story of a man totally committed to his Lord and Savior."
–Marin Garniss
Providence, Manitoulin Island, Ontario
The Peggs' pastor

Tribute
978-1-77069-585-6
Word Alive Press, 2012
To God be the Glory! It was in the late 1970s when the Walls family and Frank Macintyre of the Dundalk Herald gave Ron Pegg the opportunity of writing a weekly column for the Flesherton Advance. During the next three decades he wrote the column under a number of different names. This book includes articles from that column, along with many recent works.

Giant Among Giants: Ernest C. Manning
978-1-926676-82-1
Word Alive Press, 2010
"After sixty years of having studied Ernest C. Manning and following his career, I firmly believe that the man who was elected in seven consecutive elections as Premier of Alberta, and who never faced a close election in his entire political career, a man who still can be heard on repeat broadcasts of Canada's National Bible Broadcast, is one of Canada's greatest people."

They Call Him Garney, I Call Him Dad
978-1-926676-12-8
Word Alive Press, 2009
Garney Pegg was the owner of a small town bakery and grocery in Beeton, Ontario for almost thirty years. The business began in the first year of the Great Depression and carried on through World War II and the 1950's. He and his wife Pearl raised a family of five while facing all of the problems that a small business faced in the hazardous time of the Depression and the War.

Cow Pasture Beginnings
978-1554520497
Essence Publishing, 2006
John McGraw, in 1913, stated: "Naturally, I think baseball is the most admirable pastime in the world, a keen combination of wit, intelligence and muscle. It develops the mind, establishes discipline and gives to those who take part in it sound bodies, clear heads and a better sense of life" (The Old Ball Game, Frank Deford).

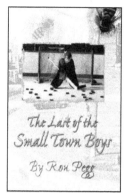

The Last of the Small Town Boys
978-1553069539
Essence Publishing, 2005
The rural village of southern Ontario where each person knew every other person, as well as each person's family history for at least three generations past, represents an era of history. Like *Anne of Green Gables, Tom Sawyer,* and *Sunshine Sketches of a Little Town* represent a time that is no more, *The Last of the Small-Town Boys* celebrates the passing of another time.

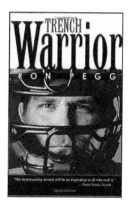

Trench Warrior
978-0884197805
Creation Books, 2001
It is said that one person can make a difference... but have you ever wondered if your life really counts? This testimony of one man's fight, his refusal to let his adversary overtake him and his trust in the orders of his Commanding Officer, will inspire and challenge you to let God use your life to accomplish great things for Him.